MILE BEHIND THE SMILE

Rediscovering Our Happiness Through Embracing Our Stories

Calvin Long

New Degree Press

Copyright © 2019 Calvin Long
All rights reserved.

ISBN   978-1-64137-312-8 *Paperback*

978-1-64137-604-4 *Ebook*

In loving memory of Grandpa Gene. A man with never-ending stories & love for our family.

To my father, who gave me his tenacity & determination to pursue any passion: the Mile.

To my mother, who gave me her caring heart & ability to love endlessly: the Smile.

For my sister Ava, who has been by my side since the day I saw you in the hospital wearing my cowboy pajamas.

CONTENTS

Introduction

———

Please take a moment to yourself to calm your mind and imagine with me for a minute. (I was going to ask you to close your eyes, but the absurdity of reading a book with your eyes closed... well, you understand!)

Imagine that instead of holding this book, you are holding the steering wheel of your car. You have your windows down as you cruise down the highway, the wind blowing, and your music blaring through your speakers. Everything seems to be perfect, no heavy traffic or construction for as far as your eyes can see. You are going your usual (*hopefully* lawful) speed, when you notice the car in front of you is going much slower than you, ruining your perfect drive.

"This person does not know how to drive" or *"why is this person in the fast lane if they are going so slow?"* are thoughts that may pop into your head. But now imagine there is a car

that speeds past you or is driving far too swiftly behind you, how dare they drive so recklessly, right? How is it that every car around you is either going too fast or too slow, and you are the only one driving at the proper speed?

Perhaps you could have perfected the right speed to be driving, but it is more likely that you are thinking in one of the many selfish mindsets we dip into as humans.[1] Just the other day, I was driving to work when I noticed a massive traffic jam in front of me.

My GPS indicated a 15-minute delay due to a crash, and my first thought was, *"Great, I just started this job last week, and I am already going to be late,"* not *"I hope the people involved were okay,"* or concerns regarding the dozens of other cars backed up. I was only concerned about myself.

* * *

"We live in a world where it has become so easy to be selfish." These words, once told to me by my friend Liz, come to mind when I am in my car.

* * *

What a strange phenomenon that as we enter our cars, it is as if we are creating a self-centered universe where everyone else is just a background character. As we turn up the music and lock the doors, all those around us seem to disappear

---

1   Berry, William. "You're So Selfish." *Psychology Today.* Sussex Publishers, April 19, 2016.

into our peripheral vision. We keep our eyes on the road, focusing only on our end destination, causing us to forget about the hundreds of people around us in their own cars and universes. In fact, we often only look over when we want to see the person who may be speeding past us or slowing us down. We may occasionally glance over and notice a woman driving slowly with a minivan full of children or a teen still learning how to work his gas and brake pedals, without scaring his parents too much with his driving. Nevertheless, our judgment overlooks their lives.

One evening, I was telling my family about how I saw a car running a red light, jumping the curb briefly in the process. At the moment, I was telling the story as a *"you will never believe what I saw today"* type of event, but my father quickly spoke up and put the storytelling on pause.

"How do you know it was a reckless driver, maybe they had an emergency, and they needed to find the closest ER?" he spoke, reminding me that, once again, not everything in life is about me.

This mindset that we find ourselves in does not only exist when we are in the comfort of our cars. Rather than having our hands wrapped around the steering wheel and our eyes focused on when to take a left turn, the roads that we drive can be a metaphor to the path of our lives. Our minds locked in and focusing on everything we need to do to hit next month's quota, pass a big exam, or achieve the goals that we have set for ourselves. In many cases, we take actions that only benefit us in order to accomplish what we have set out for, forgetting that our choices impact the lives of others. Things such as:

→ Not leaving a tip at a restaurant to save up money for vacation

→ Refusing to spend an hour a week to volunteer to have enough time to binge-watch the new episode of our favorite shows

Small choices that many of us may make without even thinking twice. But what if the waitress depended on her tips to afford food for her family, or the volunteer shelter was already running low on volunteers to cook meals for the less fortunate? We often make decisions that we think will make us happier in the long run and forget about the others who may be affected.

Seeing that choosing the option that most benefits ourselves is the most popular, and commonly easiest, I wanted to learn from those who do the opposite: who act selflessly throughout their daily interactions. These people who go out of their way to serve others, even though serving themselves can be done much more readily, have something special about them from which we can learn. Whether it is through volunteer work, advocating for self-care and seeking help, or even just simple acts of kindness, I have become inspired by those who dedicate their lives to helping others. Those who open their hearts to let others in, loved ones and strangers alike, are those who shine the brightest.

When we act selfishly, we tend to achieve a happiness that lasts only temporarily. On the other hand, we can feel the long-lasting happiness that warms our hearts and gives us purpose when we put our hearts on the line for those around us. It is in the gratitude and love expressed by others that fills our hearts with joy rather than merely acting for ourselves.

* * *

In the chapters of this book, you will read stories of people who have been able to find happiness through acts of selflessness, service, and, ultimately, love. Each chapter will revolve around a unique individual and a lesson they share with you. Through their thoughts, actions, and words, you will get a glimpse into their worldview and hear their stories. Just like the hundreds of strangers whizzing past us in cars, each person we encounter in our lives has a particular story and journey. No two people share an identical life path, offering the idea that each person who enters our lives has a valuable lesson to teach us.

Although the stories in this book do not all follow the same structure, they all have an underlying theme of how each individual was able to live life more peacefully and happily. You will read of struggles, battles, risks, and personal, vulnerable details that each person was prompted to share with the world. Why would someone allow me to write about their struggles in a book, available to any who flip the pages? I hope you will be able to answer that after getting to know some of the people and stories you will soon encounter.

This book is not going to outline "seven ways you can help others to help yourself" or suggest that you "follow these easy steps to find happiness in your life!" As much as I would like to promise you that you will find happiness by the end of the book, I cannot do that. Who am I to tell you how to define your happiness?

We all understand the concept of happiness, but that does not mean we all experience it the same way. What makes you happy is likely drastically different than what may make me feel the same sense of fulfilling joy. Why should we try to measure our happiness by comparing it with those we see around us? To help build this idea of all of us having our own, unique methods of discovering and experiencing happiness, I asked over 100 of my friends and acquaintances to tell me how and when they feel genuine, authentic happiness. Many of the responses are listed at the end of the book, but here are just a few to show the difference:

> **"I find happiness most often in the small things, like hearing a soft song coming out of the windows of a neighbor, or the quietness of the early morning. From a larger perspective, I am most happy when listening to others talk about their passions, exploring something new, cooking, and writing. I think "how" these feelings come to me is by merely feeling at peace with myself, others, and the environment I am existing in."**
>
> —MORGAN

"...When I surrounded myself with the people I love the most and those who truly, genuinely love me back. It is the small moments where everyone is present and not on phones and distracted. Human connection and good conversation."

—AMANDA

"I feel happy when I am at the gym. For me, it is a great outlet for my stress and anxiety. I also love the beach when I can go. I feel detached from the world I know and truly feel peace."

—ANONYMOUS

"When I feel happy, it is normally when I am in the full presence of another individual. Someone I can talk to, sit in silence with, have a good time with, or spend hours without getting bored. I usually experience the feeling of happiness through laughter and peace but feel it most when I am most fully present in whatever situation I may be in."

—NICHOLAS

"I experience happiness when I am engaging in any creative activity. Whether it be painting, drawing, playing guitar, acting, etc. I feel happiest when I am doing something that takes focus but is also fun. I am even happier when I do those activities with the people I love."

—ANONYMOUS

What I learned from reading through the plentiful responses were the following:

1. **A checklist of events to spend time doing, such as "spend time outdoors" or "exercise daily," may appeal to some, but it is impossible to create a 100% accurate method for us to achieve our own, personal happiness.**

2. **People want to be heard and appreciated. Merely listening to the stories people share and giving them your full attention, even for just five minutes, can mean the world to them.**

3. **No two people are precisely the same. We are all our unique selves.**

* * *

At this point, you might be wondering, "*So if this book is not going to tell me how to be happier, what is the point?*" Or even "*what makes this collection of stories different from someone else's? Why should I keep flipping through the pages?*"

The purpose of this book is not to tell you how to live your life or what changes to make to become happy. Rather than telling you what to do, this book invites you to reflect upon your life and see what is distancing you from achieving your happiness. Think of this book as a road map of the mile behind your smile, or the journey you are on to live happily and fully. This book, or map, is leading you to the goal of being able to live in happiness, sharing love from within to those around you.

And you might be thinking, "*Who needs a map to travel a mile?*" Well, we will imagine this mile is in a dark stormy wood, where a map would be necessary. Each chapter will serve as a landmark on the map, representing progress toward understanding your own sense of happiness.

Have you ever heard the phrase, "*How can you love someone else without first loving yourself?*" We can apply the same mentality to our happiness. How can you be happy with the world around you if you are not happy with yourself? This idea of internal reflection before external projection is what shaped this book, and is the mile that you will be traveling as you read.

As the stories begin, they will first discuss finding happiness through internal means, such as genuinely accepting and loving yourself, and owning your story and scars. Chapter by chapter, the stories will slowly transition from internal to external, turning your love from inward to outward. In other words, the stories reflect the progress you make while walking your mile, leading toward the end chapters that discuss finding happiness in others through service, love, and genuine connection.

By the end of the book, you will be able to look back and see where you stand in the progress of your own mile. You will understand which landmark, or story, represents a struggle that is currently preventing you from your growth. Through the lessons offered in this book, you will be able to see how at least one other person has overcome a similar obstacle.

* * *

Rather than providing you steps to achieve happiness, this book was created to remind you that you do not need to make drastic changes in your life to be happier. The stories you are about to read do not contain miraculous plots that could have an award-winning movie made about them. Instead, each chapter tells the story of a human being who is simply an ordinary person. This concept serves as a reminder that the battles you read about in this book not only exist in these pages but also are very real in the lives of many. Although I attach a name to each story, the struggles within the story could be affecting someone you know: a friend, family member, classmate, or even you. For example, these are a few of the themes that you will soon be familiar with as you continue to read:

→ A girl weighed down by anxiety
→ A woman forced to start over after a divorce
→ An adult struggling to find his or her purpose in life
→ A friend trying to find strength to overcome an eating disorder
→ A victim of bullying feeling silenced

Sound familiar? If so, let this book be a reminder that you are not going through your hardships alone, and your pain is not permanent. Although some stories will be riddled with hurt, they all show that even in the lowest of lows, it is possible to rise up and flourish.

As you read through this book, I ask of you to not feel compelled to compare yourself with anyone who is telling their story. Although you may see parts of yourself in some of the stories, remember that you are unique, just as they are. Similar to how we all define and find happiness in our own, unique ways, we all cope and find solutions that best fit ourselves. It is not selfish to try to discover your own means of happiness and self-worth. We must recognize that there is a fine line between being selfish and self-aware. Keep this in mind as you continue reading.

We all have stories to tell and wisdom to offer. I ask you to approach each story with the same mentality, listening to the individual's journey to finding a genuine, selfless form of happiness. Through each chapter and story, including my own, I hope you are able to recognize the sentiment in each page and are reminded of the love that resides around and within you.

How to Use This Book

———

Treat this book as if it were a map, with each chapter acting as a landmark you want to see before you reach your destination. Sometimes maps can be confusing, which is why I wanted to give you a few tips on how to use this book as your map:

Stop at each Landmark

If you are taking a road trip from New York to California, what would you rather do?

→ Drive all 2,900 miles straight through without stopping
→ Stop at the attractions or landmarks along the way

Now I know it is cliché to say that *"it is not the destination; it is the journey,"* but I am sure it is okay to say regarding books. Each landmark, or chapter, will play an essential role in the natural progression of the book. An important lesson throughout this book is to not judge a book by its cover, and I ask you to maintain this mentality while approaching each story. If you skip ahead, you might miss out on an attraction that could be your favorite!

Follow the Course of the Map

I would suggest reading the book from beginning to end, each chapter in order. Not correctly following a map can get you lost, and the last thing I would want is for you to feel lost in these pages. Although each chapter contains its own story, it is essential to read them in order and witness the progression from internal to external happiness.

Customize Your Reading Journey

There are still plenty of ways to make this book, indeed, **your** book. Now that it is in your hands, you can treat it however you would like.

→ **Mark it like a journal.** I know when I read books, I always sit with my highlighter next to me, ready to high-light any passage or quote that resonates with me.

→ **Fold it like a textbook.** Find a page you really like? Fold the corner and come back to it later!

→ **Grip it like a steering wheel.** Keep your eyes glued to the pages as if they were the road ahead of you, or read casually; it is totally up to you!

Make Plans to Road Trip Again

Some people only like to make road trips once and then move on to another adventure. I hope that you find at least one chapter you enjoy enough to flip back to and read again.

Buckle Up and Enjoy!

Before you start this book and read the stories, please ask yourself these three questions. Feel free to write your responses anywhere on this page, for I will ask you to come back and compare your answers after you have read the last page of this book.

1. **What is your personal definition of happiness?**
2. **What is preventing you from taking this definition and turning it into reality?**
3. **How can you overcome this obstacle?**

Take a moment to think, reflect, and respond. Calm your mind and reflect on your life and yourself, both past, present, and future. When you feel at peace with your answers, let us start this journey together.

Part One:
SOCIETY

Chapter 1:
Happiness

Nothing says the first day of school like carrying a backpack full of unopened school supplies, wearing new clothes that are doomed to get dirty at recess, and telling the entire class about yourself.

"Please tell us your name, favorite food, and one fun fact about yourself that we can remember you by" is a question I have been asked in just about every new classroom I walked into, from kindergarten up to my final year of college.

Year after year, my answer was always the same, as if nothing had changed since the prior year. (And in case you were wondering, the answer is "Calvin, pizza, and I am a triplet"). Although we as human beings are constantly changing, it seemed that the questions asked to us never do. Like many others, I believed that ice breakers were just an initial way of putting off school work until the second day because, honestly, nobody was actually going to remember your dog's name or your love for hamburgers.

My friend Anna recently introduced me to a question that made me reconsider my opinion of ice breakers: "What are you most excited for or happy about in your life right now?" Unlike your favorite food or a secret talent that you have, this answer could change by the year, month, or even hour. In the blink of an eye, you could receive an email offering you the dream job you interviewed for or get a text from an old friend that you had been missing.

I would like for you to take this moment and think about the one event, piece of news, conversation, or anything that you are happy about in your life right now. Think back to a week ago, three months ago, and even last year. Is your answer the same?

Odds are most likely not, because our happiness in life is not static; it grows and changes at the same rate that we do. When I was a child, my mother used to have our family write in a journal each school year, filling out questions such as our favorite subject, the new friends we have made, and what we wanted to be when we grew up, similar to the common icebreaker questions. As a twenty-two-year-old, I flip through these pages and reminisce about the world in which I lived. Each new year had a new dream occupation, from an artist to a teacher, and even a baseball player, despite never playing a baseball game outside the limits of our backyard. Year after year, my interests and hobbies changed, as did what brought me happiness. Although many of these aspirations had just been silly things for me to write down on the first and last days of school, I believe they offer insight into us as human beings.

* * *

**"If I could see the world through the eyes of
a child, what a wonderful world this would be."**

—PATSY CLINE

Children view the world through a special lens that offers visions of joy and wonder. The possibilities are endless when looking through this lens, but as we grow older, the lens becomes smudged and foggy with experience and reality. Some may say that we lose this love for life as we age because we become aware of the world in which we live. As we grow older, we continue to take on more and more responsibilities, the stress replacing the happiness we once had. We feel ourselves naturally comparing our characteristics to those around us, even subconsciously. Our appearance, success, wardrobe, paycheck, and happiness all become different measures for us to rank how we are doing in life against those around us. From trying to fit in at school to the never-ending process of trying to outperform other competitors at work, we feel the weight of wanting to be better.

In fact, there is a phenomenon called the "Happiness U Curve" that shows the average life satisfaction as we age. The graph demonstrates that our happiness tends to decline once we hit the age of 20, and the only time for it to begin curving back upwards is near the age of retirement.[2] The clear message

---

2   Paresky, Pamela B. "Miserable and Middle-Aged? Is Something Wrong with You?" *Psychology Today*. Sussex Publishers, April 27, 2018.

that this graph depicts is the fact that from the time we start working until the very last day on the job, the average person is on a downward spiral regarding their happiness. Whether it is from the constant stress of work, added responsibilities of raising a family, or becoming financially independent, life is just not as enjoyable.

The main takeaway I commonly see of this graph is to show us that it is okay for us to be unhappy at work, everyone else is too! Except, is it really okay? It is fair to say that, yes, we cannot be happy every second of every day. However, should we be promoting the idea that it is okay to settle in life? Just because you see a statistic in *Forbes* that says 52.3% of people are unhappy at work[3], does not mean you should allow yourself to normalize this feeling of dreading Mondays. Although work may consume around nine hours of our day, it does not dictate our entire life.

We are the drivers controlling the direction our lives will take. Whether you follow a spiritual guiding light or have a gut instinct that urges you to act, ultimately, you are the one writing the manuscript of your life story. Research shows that adults make approximately 35,000 decisions a day, both consciously and subconsciously.[4] Whether it is true or not, we face decisions from the moment we wake up until

3   Sturt, David, and Todd Nordstrom. "10 Shocking Workplace Stats You Need To Know." *Forbes*. Forbes Magazine, March 8, 2018.

4   Hoomans, Joel. *35,000 Decisions: The Great Choices of Strategic Leaders*. 35,000 Decisions: The Great Choices of Strategic Leaders. Roberts Wesleyan College, March 20, 2015

the very seconds before we fall asleep, all to repeat this cycle in just a few short hours. Although many of these choices and decisions are routine, they have an impact on our life. One decision leads to another, creating a cascading chain of events. The point? If you are feeling yourself getting stuck in an unhappy environment, alter a choice you make day after day. No, waking up 15 minutes earlier to do a morning run or deciding to smile at your coworkers as you walk past them will not instantly make your life perfect, but it could lead to a chain reaction that leads to an improvement.

"*Choose happiness*" is a motto that might come to your mind when confronted with the idea of making a decision. However, like so many others on this planet, you will know that utterly "choosing" to be happy is not that easy. Sometimes this advice of "altering your mindset to recognize the good in your life" can be ignorant of the issue at hand. People who are struggling in life are not able to quickly flip a switch in their brain and see the world through rose-colored glasses, or the lens of children mentioned earlier.

Years upon years of hardship and battles, often faced alone, leave scars that cannot heal with only a Band-aid of "try thinking positive thoughts." This is what often makes it so difficult for others to accurately prescribe a solution to find happiness through blogs, books, schedules, and countless other methods. I fully understand that I am not going to be the one to turn your life around, for that is not my job, but rather yours.

In the chapters that follow, you will hear stories of people sharing their vulnerable battles and how they were able to find happiness in themselves and the world around them. They will share their stories and struggles, and we will see how they were able to rediscover the joy in their lives, offering examples and guidance for those who are willing to listen.

However, before we dive into the lives of those that follow, here are a few more questions to keep in mind as you read.

→ Why does society present this idea of happiness as a fleeting memory from our childhood?

→ Why are there so many books written about achieving happiness as if it is not something that many people experience every day?

I believe that we live in a society where it has become too natural for us to fall short of the expectations set out for us. For example, I would like you to imagine yourself around a table, catching up briefly with friends or family who you have not seen for several years. Despite knowing you very little, they seem to have no problem asking you cliché questions about your life, career ambitions, relationship status, and personal decisions you may have made. As you try to eat your food and have a peaceful evening, all you can hear are questions such as:

→ "Why have you not found that dream job yet?"

→ "You are still single? My neighbor, who is your age, got married three years ago!"

→ "Why would you get that tattoo? Nobody will hire you when they see that!"

In this scenario, these questions from distant acquaintances represent the expectations and pressures society places on people to achieve happiness. Stories of people who are much more successful are surrounding us wherever we go. Whether it be from social media, the news, or a passing remark at the dinner table, we cannot escape.

These expectations have existed for many years, slowly crafting a picture-perfect image of living the American dream. This concept of the perfect life suggests that everyone should aim to have a happy family in peaceful suburbia, where everyone drives to their dream job at 7:00 AM and returns home to their loving partner and adorable children. Although it promotes happy living and a healthy relationship with your family, this happiness from achieving the American dream is outdated, causing harm to those who feel themselves struggling to reach it, ultimately falling short.

Society tells us that we can find happiness in material things and a big house. However, we can become so lost in our drive to *earn* more that we forget to *be* more.

→ More *loving* to our family members
→ More *connected* with our friends
→ More spiritually *centered*
→ More *engaged* with the world around us

The relationships that we cultivate throughout our lives create a more lasting impact than a hefty paycheck. Often when we find ourselves feeling lost in the world, we become less loving, connected, centered, and engaged. In these moments, what will pull you back up to your feet? The money in your pocket, or the hands of others? Our money in the bank does not define our self-worth, nor should our happiness be measured by it.

I invite you to put this idea to the test by using the icebreaker question discussed earlier when you feel a lull in conversation. Alternatively, better yet, ask people who are on opposite ends of the happiness curve, such as your grandparents. They have lived long lives, experienced happiness in many different forms, shapes, and sizes. Do you think their answers will be their high-paying jobs they retired from, or will it be something much different? There is only one way to find out: by listening. Hear their stories and how society has shaped them. How have they been able to find happiness through their many years on this planet?

Before you turn the page, take time to think about your answer to this question:

What are you most excited for or happy about in your life right now?

Chapter 2:
Perfection

Happiness is not perfection. A common misconception about being happy is that the most satisfied people tend to have everything going for them in their lives: the perfect house, perfect family, perfect job, and just a perfect life in general. What this drive for a perfect life might bring you is material happiness, lasting only in the short run. It is like a child getting everything he or she asked for on their Christmas list. They fill up a piece of paper with all the hottest new toys and hope to unwrap the colorful paper on Christmas day to find them. However, in all honesty, how long will this child be satisfied with these new gifts? Will they play with them for years and years, or will they fill up another list with entirely different toys just a year later?

This *"perfect"* Christmas day feeling of getting everything you wanted wrapped up and under a tree is not how we should be seeking happiness. Even as adults, we continue to want better and newer cars, clothes, jewelry, and other items that will put a smile on our faces but not fill our hearts. I mean, this is not truly fulfilling. What happens when you do not get the gift you wanted or if something does not go your way? Does the smile you once had fade away? If so, then what you were searching for is likely not a genuine sense of happiness.

When looking at vocabulary.com, being happy is described as "a feeling of joy, pleasure, or good fortune — exactly how you would feel if you learned that you won the lottery or got accepted into your number one choice of colleges."[5] Which is undoubtedly true; these actions would make many of us happy, but once again, for how long?

This dilemma brings up a two-sided concept of what happiness may be to some people. Yes, happiness can be viewed as the warm, fuzzy feeling inside our chests when we receive something pleasant, such as a gift or acceptance into a college. However, it is imperative to look at ourselves from the opposite perspective: how we react when we do not get these luxuries. For if a person were genuinely happy and at peace with his/her life, missing out on a big opportunity would be upsetting, but it would not create a lasting negative impact on the person. In other words, happiness can be the ability to find the light in life even when you are surrounded by darkness. From the Christmas example earlier, which child do you think is living a happier life, the one who pouts about not getting what they asked for, or the one grateful for the other gifts they have received? In this view, happiness is rooted in one's heart, rather than their smile.

---

5   "Happiness — Dictionary Definition." Vocabulary.com. 2019.

The heart will play a significant role in the telling of these stories, as it does in our lives. Like the concept of happiness, the heart also has two components that I would like to discuss. The first being a *"happy heart."* We have all heard the phrase *"my heart is so happy"* or *"bursting with joy,"* which symbolizes that the person is feeling overwhelmed with happiness. A person with a happy heart can be seen wearing a beaming smile, and you can practically feel the positivity radiating out of them as they speak. They are willing to share the love they have within them to those around them, a sheer sign of happiness.

However, the heart can be more than just happy; it can also be strong. Technically, our heart is a muscular organ that pumps blood throughout our body.[6] However, I would like you to imagine it as if it were any other muscle in your body for now.

As bodybuilders lift weights and push their bodies to their limits, their muscles are torn and rebuilt even bigger and stronger. Our hearts are the same. As humans, we put our hearts through so much distress, some more than others. Those who have had their hearts broken and suffered immense pain have the option to allow their hearts to repair and become stronger. We grow from the pain we endure; those who have the biggest hearts are often the ones who have suffered the most and have been able to grow from this pain. Sometimes it seems impossible to overcome what drags you down when your heart feels shattered beyond repair. However, it is nothing

---

6   How the Heart Works." National Heart Lung and Blood Institute. U.S. Department of Health and Human Services.

you cannot overcome. Do not let a tear in your heart be what stops you from getting out of bed. Instead, let it fuel you to become stronger.

It is not to say that suffering causes us to be happy, because that certainly is not true. We do not need to undergo pain and suffering to find happiness, but it bears us an opportunity that we generally fail to notice. Happiness is not commonly linked to overcoming dark times and struggles in our lives. Society typically broadcasts the final version of happiness, the perfect house, life, and job, but very rarely show the journey that took place beforehand to reach this level.

Kindness is also commonly assumed to be a result of living happily and perfectly. Those who are happy are also kind. No shock there, right? Earlier this year, I saw the following quote that stopped me in my tracks, making me rethink my rationale as to why people are so kind to others.

> **"Some of the kindest souls I know have lived in a world that was not so kind to them. Some of the best human beings I know have been through so much at the hands of others, and they still love deeply, they still care. Sometimes, it is the people who have been hurt the most who refuse to be hardened in this world, because [they] would never want to make another person feel the same way they have felt."**
> —BIANCA SPARACINO[7]

---

7   Sparacino, Bianca. *The Strength in Our Scars*. Thought Catalog, 2017.

Rather than saying that people who have lived perfectly are the happiest, this quote suggests rather the complete opposite: the people who have been torn down, pushed to their limits, and had their hearts tested day after day are the kindest and happiest. This idea goes to show that there are two ways to react to such pain and struggling. We can be selfish and dwell in the hurt, focusing only on how we feel and how we can fix ourselves. Alternatively, we can be kind, taking our pain, and doing our best to prevent it from happening to others like us. A single choice in how we react to our distress can create such a lasting impact on not only our lives but also in the lives of others.

However, people commonly do not openly discussed this idea when the topic of happiness is brought up. Why? Simply put, the concept of suffering is not as glamorous as posting about material wealth and happiness. It is much easier to discuss the positive aspects of your life and post photos of you smiling. There is often a negative stigma when opening up about not being "okay." People might start looking at you weird, trying to analyze your behavior and view you differently. That being said, sometimes, it can feel embarrassing to become so vulnerable about your past.

Remember the nerves you felt in school when it was your turn to stand in front of the class and talk about some book you were asked to read? Well, imagine this feeling, but the presentation script and PowerPoint slides behind you are about the details of the hardest times in your life. To me, this would be much harder than giving a presentation on *Huckleberry Finn*. You are stripping down the walls you had built up to hide this past, exposing the part of your life that weighed you down for so long.

However, once again, how does this make us happier?

Perhaps it is the feeling of the burden being lifted, not having to hide this part of your life anymore. Maybe it is the final step of conquering your past, feeling strong enough to claim your victory and to finally put an end to the struggles. Or, it could relate to the idea of finding happiness in helping others. Sharing your story might be the reason why someone decides to seek professional help, speak up to their parents about an issue, or understand that they are not alone in what they are going through. Those who endure pain allow for their hearts to break and rebuild stronger, allowing their love to spread to those around them who may be lacking love. Possibly this sense of providing support will enable them to find their purpose in life, to act as a guiding light. Though, that is for you to discover through their words and stories.

* * *

Happiness is not perfection. I struggled with this belief for many years, as did the others who share their peace later in this book. It was stories like theirs that encouraged me to write this book because I knew if expanding the idea of what it means to be happy could help me, it could help others. They made the decision not to hide their past, no matter how dark or imperfect it may be, creating a narrative and offering us all a lesson. To stay true to this message of not fearing your past, I challenged myself to discuss my struggles within these pages as well, something I have never done before.

As the stories begin, they will discuss finding happiness through internal means, such as genuinely accepting one's self and finding the love from within themselves. Each story takes part in creating a path, leading toward the last chapters, which discuss finding happiness in others through service, love, and genuine connection. I ask you to avoid measuring yourself to the teller of each story, but to ask yourself:

→ What can I gain from each story?
→ How can I use this to expand my existing idea of what it means to find peace and be happy?

But first, there is one last societal pressure that constrains our happiness that needs to be addressed. Any guesses what it could be? Turn the page, and you will soon find out.

Chapter 3:
"Social"

———

Being viewed as "perfect" has always been a societal pressure, but it has grown immensely in the digital age.

We live in a world where becoming connected with others is as easy as the touch of a screen. Social media has *united* us in the twenty-first century, allowing us to grow our social connections as we follow, friend, connect, and tag our friends on a wide variety of platforms. It has almost become a requirement of our society to have social media if we want to remain connected with our distant friends and family members. In that sense of staying connected, social media has made a positive impact. But is this connection actually making us more social with our network, or is it just deepening the divide that stands between us?

* * *

I have always viewed my cell phone as a security blanket that I can carry around with me. Any time I feel myself looking for a way to pass the time or avoid awkward silences, I can pull out my phone and immerse myself in the hours of entertainment offered at just the touch of a screen. Also, being able to check up on friends and family through texting and the many social media platforms makes me feel more connected.

All this incredible technology, how could anyone complain about it? I know it can be easy to disregard the complaints from the older generation about teens and young adults being addicted and glued to their phones these days. I remember I would always roll my eyes and continue scrolling on my screen as my mother would complain about the hours I spend on my phone.

"These older adults never grew up with this technology, of course, they are not going to understand the power it has" is something I would often say to myself. However, I would soon learn I was partially right, that technology does have great power... power **over** us.

What was once a security blanket turned into an attachment, even an addiction that I was not willing to admit. I would like you to briefly reflect on your day and try to count how many times you have looked at your phone. Was it the first thing you looked at in the morning, or the last thing you used at night? A study done by Deloitte reported that the average American checks their phone forty-six times a day, while the average 17–24-year-old American will check an average of seventy-four times a day.[8] A bit higher than

---

8   Eadicicco, Lisa. "Americans Check Their Phones 8 Billion Times Per Day." *Time*. Time, December 15, 2015.

you were expecting, right? The fact of the matter is that this addiction is not the only problem, but rather it stems deeper into our personal lives.

Social media, at first, seems like a beautiful idea, especially to young adults. We can keep up to date with friends that we might not be able to see very often, see posts from those we look up to, and even update others on our own lives. But, as we continue returning to social media, day after day, we become more and more hooked on it. It is truly a wolf in sheep's clothing. From a distance, it appears to be an excellent method to remain social, but as it draws us in, we begin to question it. Then, it is too late, the wolf that is social media consumes us figuratively, mentally, and emotionally.

We can find ourselves scrolling through content for hours, our eyes and fingers glued to the screen. It becomes so easy to forget about our reality when we have access to look into the "*lives*" of so many others. However, what we so easily forget is that the "*lives*" people share on social media are just the best moments they are willing to showcase. We can even find ourselves wanting to post only positive updates or happy photos of us to maintain this picture-perfect life to show others. This then creates a sense of being faced with unrealistic expectations from these inauthentic lives that others share.

With our screens full of photos of others from fun vacations, their expensive clothing and cars, and perfect bodies, it is just human nature to wonder, *"why am I not as skinny, famous, pretty, popular?"* Our lives can feel small compared to the many others we expose ourselves to every day; we forget about the good we have and crave to be better. Feelings of loneliness, lowered self-esteem and self-worth, insecurities about our appearance, and wanting attention from others soon flood our brains as we become swallowed by social media.

Rather than continuing to bombard you with statistic after statistic about the adverse effects social media has on our happiness, I have collected short reflections from college students discussing their personal experience with social media. Following each will be a brief statistic to validate the sentiment they share.

"I was always an anxious and insecure child as I was growing up. However, when social media came into my life in middle and high school, my insecurities grew. This led my anxiety to grow, and I felt that I always needed to please every single person around me. I wanted everyone to like me, and I was afraid that I was doing something wrong when someone did not. Social media has not only added insecurities to my life but has continued to impact my already strained mental health negatively."

—ABBY P

60% of people using social media reported that it had impacted their self-esteem in a negative way[9]

> "Social media, first and foremost, takes my attention away from whatever I am experiencing at that moment. When I am with friends, it can take me away from the gift of their presence. When I am alone, it takes my focus away from me and the goals I need to accomplish that day. Social media also makes it very easy for me to compare myself to the lives of others. As much as I try to live my life with my values, it is hard to do that when I see my friends or people I look up to posting their most exciting life events on social media."
>
> —NICHOLAS C

Facebook usage was directly related to both less moment-to-moment happiness and less life satisfaction: The more people used Facebook in a day, the more these two variables decreased.[10]

> "Social media has taken a toll on every area of my health and has for everyone, in my opinion. Whether or not we like to admit it, social media has

---

9   Silva, Clarissa. "Social Media's Impact on Self-Esteem." *HuffPost*. HuffPost, February 22, 2017.

10 Kross, Ethan, Philippe Verduyn, Emre Demiralp, David Seungjae Lee, Natalie Lin, Holly Shablack, John Jonides, and Oscar Ybarra. "Facebook Use Predicts Declines in Subjective Well-Being in Young Adults." PLOS ONE. Public Library of Science, August 14, 2013.

made it a daily requirement to compare yourself to everyone else. Wake up, compare yourself to others, eat lunch, compare yourself to others, eat dinner, get ready for bed, compare yourself to others, fall asleep, repeat. Whether it boosts one's self-esteem or not, constantly seeing where you fall compared to others will never end well. In some cases, we have a heightened sense of our worth, but in most cases, we have an extremely lowered sense of self-worth. This lack of worth spirals into many mental health issues and caring too much, or not at all, about your well-being."

—REGINA S

Compared to students who scarcely use social media, those who do use it regularly experience much higher levels of fear of missing out, loneliness, anxiety, depression, lower self-esteem, and lower self-acceptance.[11]

"Social media takes time away from things that I love to do, feeling obligated to constantly check it even though there is nothing substantial on it. Social media negatively impacts my mental health by making me question if I am doing things "right." Social media makes me question

---

11 Hunt, Melissa G, Rachel Marx, Courtney Lipson, and Jordyn Young. "No More FOMO: Limiting Social Media Decreases Loneliness and Depression." *Journal of Social and Clinical Psychology*, 2018

things I do to the point that I always have to
delete Snapchat and Instagram from my phone
to feel less constrained. I believe social media
is the worst thing to happen to mental health."

—EMMA B

"Too much passive use of social media — just browsing
posts — can be unhealthy and has been linked to feelings
of envy, inadequacy, and less satisfaction with life. Studies
have even suggested that it can lead to ADHD symptoms,
depression, anxiety, and sleep deprivation."[12]

"For one, it is very addicting and affects my sleep
schedule all the time. My most productive days are
the days when I am not able to access my phone
and such. I often see things on social media that
are inaccurately portrayed, and then I wish I was
doing that or was different based on what I saw"

—CHRIS S

72% of people sleep with their phone in their bed or within
reach, causing late-night distractions and sleep-loss.[13]

"The most prominent way has been body image
for me. It is hard to see "perfect" girls every
day, and it gives an unrealistic expectation to

---

12 Fersko, Henry. "Is Social Media Bad for Teens' Mental Health?"
    UNICEF, October 9, 2018.
13 "How Technology Impacts Sleep Quality." Sleep.org.

"normal" girls (I know everyone is beautiful in their own way, but self-doubt creeps in at times)

—MAEVE M

88% of women said they compare themselves to images on social media, with only 13% of the comparison being positive. [14]

I feel as though I am "addicted" to social media. I am on it a lot and sometimes for long periods of time. I think it negatively impacts my mental health because I always know there are other ways I can spend my time more efficiently. Sometimes I can get upset or feel lonely when I see people hanging out on social media, and I am alone.

—ABBY C

Nearly 50% of college students spend between 2 to 5 hours each day on social media, distancing themselves from those around them.[15]

These respondents, as well as the 80 others, represent a demographic that grew up in this culture of being surrounded by social media. The words, shared by each individual, should offer more insight than those who grew up before social media became a cultural norm or necessity to stay connected. Out of

---

14 "#Bodypositive: A Look at Body Image & Social Media." FHE Health — Addiction & Mental Health Care. FHE Health, November 30, 2017.

15 Society, American Physiological. "Though Distracted by Social Media, Students Are Still Listening." Though distracted by social media, students are still listening. Phys.org, April 13, 2018.

the eighty-seven responses, a mere four of them discussed how social media has not been harmful to them in any way, less than five percent. But that does not stop us from continuing our habits. It has become part of our nature to pick up our phones and scroll through each social media app for hours, consuming content that does more harm than good.

It is a dilemma of dampening our happiness with such an easy, routine task that is at the tip of our fingers. However, a handful of the responses went into detail about how freeing it was to turn off their phones or delete their social media apps. When I went on an immersion experience to El Salvador for around a week, our phones had been locked up in a safe to keep us engaged in the experience. This feeling of being free from my phone allowed me to enjoy the company of all those around me genuinely.

However, it just is not practical to lock our phones in a safe in our everyday lives. A friend of mine, Morgan M, recently told me about how she decided to delete the Instagram app from her phone. In her mind, it was not a tough decision to make, yet many others had asked her if it were hard to go through the day without it. Although the sentiment of checking on her was appreciated, what does it say about our society that deleting a social media app can be viewed as a big deal or a challenge to us? After going through life for several months, she felt the urge to reconnect on social media due to the sense of feeling disconnected from her friends. What this creates is a fine line between being able to use social media to feel connected to others while not falling into the dark hole of self-comparison, jealousy, and loneliness that is so commonly attached to social media.

So, what could be the solution? Well, we cannot cut out social media entirely from our lives to become happy. Instead, we need to reevaluate the ways that we use social media and the values we seek from it. Rather than following people who make you feel the need to compare yourself, follow those who inspire and motivate you. Communicate with those who lift you up rather than tear you down. Share posts that radiate the love and support you would want to give to your friends and family. Budget your time like you do with expenses, not spending too much time each day on social media. Try to let social media be a source of inspiration, not negativity.

Social media was not created to have such a harmful impact, but society has allowed these adverse side effects to become more and more prevalent. However, we can find the good in social media, choosing to use it to lift ourselves up and genuinely feel *united* with others.

Chapter 4:
Unity

———

While I was in middle school, our school district would pick a different phrase to act as a tagline for that school year. At this age, these new taglines meant very little to me. Rather than buying a shirt with this new phrase on it once a year, twelve-year-old me did very little to even think about what each tagline meant. Like typical pre-teens, I was too distracted by trying to pick out the coolest colors for my braces or buying the right clothes to fit in. Truthfully, there is only one phrase that has stuck with me throughout all my years at school: "Unity in Our Community."

Looking back on this phrase nearly ten years later, it resonates with me in a way I never would have imagined. Initially, the slogan *"unity in our community"* was created to unite all the families who attend the school district to develop a sense of school spirit. By flooding the bleachers with purple and gold on a cold Friday night, the goal was successful: they created unity. However, under all the face paint and the loud cheers, how truly connected were we? Yes, we all belong to the same school district, but this is not necessarily by our own decision. For many students, we had no choice but to be united with the students around us; they were just placed in our lives for twelve years based on where our parents decided to raise us.

However, this inauthentic unity does not come from the school itself; I love the school district where I grew up. Instead, it was the way of life many of us lived while we are coasting through school at a young age. Throughout these years in our lives, we tend to live selfishly, which takes away from wanting genuine unity with others. We tend to get so caught up in our own personal interests that we forget about those around us. The importance of dressing well and having the most fashionable haircut to make us fit in would often overshadow the feelings of other people.

But what happens when families cannot afford to buy more expensive clothing to help their child "fit in" at school? This creates a more-defined line between the middle-class and lower-income families, creating more opportunities for exclusion. This exclusion may stem bullying and mistreating others based on their material clothing, creating an even lesser form of unity.

Along with trying our best to fit in, eight hours of school, piles of homework, sports, and other extracurricular activities consume the majority of our lives. This packed schedule leaves very little time to unite with all those around you. Even at events where students do come together, like sporting events and pep rallies, they could be in a crowd of unfamiliar faces, questioning the real authenticity of their community. We find comfort in familiarity, making it easier to surround ourselves with those we know and do not attempt to get to know those we do not know. However, this mindset does not stick with us for the rest of our lives, we mature, and we grow.

As a recent senior in college, the phrase "unity in our community" sits differently in my heart than it did initially ten years ago. It should not come as a shock that a college student and a middle school student have two very different perspectives on life. An apparent cause could be that life is much different for a twelve and twenty-two-year-old. College students tend to live very differently than those younger and older than they. They are quickly forced to learn to live independently. This shift leads to much self-discovery and learning to appreciate others for who they are, not how they dress.

Of course, there are the stereotypical stories of those who attend college to take up a life of partying without parental supervision. But that is just one example of how college opens the door to truly living your life as you wish. There are countless opportunities in which to engage, learning about the world, the community around you, and yourself. To better understand what commonly brings college students together, I turned to a man named Jamie, who works with college students to better unite them on campus.

Jamie first started his career working with college students in fraternities and sororities, specifically in peer advisory and risk management of the Greek life organizations. After working in this department at several universities, Jamie discovered that there was one feature of every job that made him feel fulfilled: the well-being of students. Although he thought he was successful working with the Greek life organizations, he wanted to specialize more in helping students directly and making an impact in their lives. This lead to his current position, as a wellness director, where he works with students every day to develop different campaigns and events to help students improve their well-being. Whether it is physical fitness, healthy eating, mental health, or substance abuse, he strives to help the students in the university's community.

A recent campaign that has united the college campus is called "Work in Progress," created with the help of a student named John Tucci, which brings attention to being open about your mental health and to normalizes seeking help. With this campaign, students who participate are asked to become vulnerable to their community by talking about their struggles. Each participant gets their own poster and is asked, "What are you struggling with?" and "How do you deal with and overcome this struggle?"

The main objective is to show the students around campus that the friendly faces they see walking the crowded halls with a smile may be dealing with an internal battle; they are a work in progress. By listing activities that these participants engage in to lessen their struggle, it urges others who may be feeling the same way to find ways to cope as well.

After meeting with students who wanted to participate in this campaign, Jamie was able to notice that they all shared a common theme that made them feel connected to the idea: *a deep connection to the community.* In college, you start and end the day, surrounded by the same people. You constantly interact with people within the campus seven days a week for around nine months out of the year for four years. When you do the math, that is a lot of time to be around the same group of people, especially when the campus is relatively small. You begin to learn the names of just about everyone you see walking in the halls. Through these constant interactions, you can watch those around you grow and change into their true authentic selves. These strangers you met four years ago become people who you could not imagine living without; they become part of your family. And like family, you never want to see someone you love suffering.

These students felt called to open up about their struggles to help other students overcome their own. If your brother or sister were struggling with a breakup, you would want to be there for them and promise them that everything gets better, right? This mindset is what college students tend to have, except their "family" extends outward to include the community where they live. Although a battle through mental health may be personal and leave deep scars in your heart, sharing it with those around you may offer guidance in their struggle.

As you continue reading, you will discover that many people speak up about their past to remind others that no matter where they may be in their life, it is not permanent. You could be at the bottom of the ocean with anchors around your ankles, but that is not your destiny. The lowest point in life is not lasting; it will get better. This is tough to comprehend when you are the one drowning in your thoughts, but sometimes seeing someone you love open up about how they survived a similar situation can be the first step necessary to recovery.

As we get older, the urgency to fit in with those around us withers away. Putting on a disguise and acting like the person you want others to think you are is inauthentic. In college, you leave this idea of portraying the perfect life in the past. You will soon discover that people will embrace you regardless of who you are, no matter what imperfections you may have.

As author Brené Brown once said, "Imperfections are not inadequacies; they are reminders that we are all in this together."[16] This quote is something I have learned through my four years of college, the fact that not a single soul around you is living a perfect life. Everyone is fighting a unique battle; some are just better at hiding it than others.

---

16 Brown, Brené. "The Power of Vulnerability." YouTube. Ted, January 3, 2011.

The unity felt in college that lacks in our younger years is not merely from just becoming more mature; it is from being our true selves. People will love you for you, not the mask you put on or façade you show on social media. When everyone around you is not afraid to let their true colors shine through like a kaleidoscope, there is genuine unity in the community.

Part Two:
STORIES

The Stories

———

I invite you into the lives of all those willing to tell their stories in the following pages. Each chapter will be detailing the story of one individual, depicting the mile behind their smile. Just like running the mile run in gym class, I ask of you to read at your own pace. There is no need to rush through each story, for blurring of the stories and their details may occur.

Each chapter is its own individual story, unlike a fictional book chapter that shares the same plot from beginning to end. However, that is not to say that they are unrelated. The chapters will guide you down a path, starting with stories that discuss finding happiness within yourself. Chapter by chapter, the storytellers will transition from finding and accepting love from within to finding happiness through external means, such as service and acts of kindness. This progression is to show that in order to be authentically happy and share our love with those around us, we must first love ourselves.

At the end of each chapter, there will be a page for reflection. This page will differ from chapter to chapter, posing different questions for you to reflect on based on what you had just read. I promise it is not a quiz to see if you were paying attention, but an opportunity for you to take a moment and think about what you read. Allowing time in between each chapter may allow for the details to resonate more with you, letting them settle into your mind and heart before jumping into the next. You can write the answers down in the book, in a journal, or just let the topic reside in your mind for a few moments. This is your book, and you get to choose how you use it and how it helps you.

Along with each reflection page, there will be a song listed for your ears. This idea originated from a retreat I once participated in, and then helped lead the following year. Taking three minutes to close your eyes and focus on nothing but the music allows for great peace, but also moments for reflection. I have learned that music plays such an essential role in my life, allowing me to feel my emotions deeper through the lyrics I hear.

There are instances where a person will reference a song lyric in their story. To avoid copyright law infringement by including the actual lyrics, I ask of you to listen to the song for yourself instead. At the end of the book, I will include a list of all the songs, as well as other songs that inspired me throughout writing this book.

The idea to mix this musical reflection within the pages of this book also came from my friend Katie O'Connell. She recently wrote her own book titled *Live LIVE!*, a book about creating communities in music experiences.[17] Alongside the

_____

17   O'Connell, Katie. *Live LIVE!* New Degree Press, 2019.

book, she created a playlist throughout the stories she told. I loved the idea, so thank you, Katie.

Lastly, always remember that every one of us has our own unique stories and remedies. These stories are not told for you to compare yourself to the speaker, but rather to take in their words and use them in a manner most beneficial to you. This book is not designed to tell you precisely what you need to do to become happy, but I do hope you find something meaningful and helpful from the words of each story.

Sit back, relax, and get ready for the first mile.

ODE TO THE LIBRARY

A library can be quiet
While books collect dust,
Often avoided by all
Unless studying is a must.
These quiet halls
With book after book,
Remind me to embrace life
And the journey I have took
Like books in a row
Waiting patiently to be read,
All those you encounter
Have a story in their head.
Every book you read
And each person you meet,
Offers you a lesson
To make your heart skip a beat.
From the kind new friend
Who showed you her heart,
To those you've known
Ever since the very start.
Their love lines their hearts
Like words on a page,
Ready to be shared
And break through the cage.
Like books filling a shelf
There is love all around,
Reminding you every day
That happiness can be found.

by Calvin Long

Chapter 5:
Calvin

"You are confined only by the walls you build yourself"

—ANDREW MURPHY

Road trips can be pretty awkward if you are traveling with someone you barely know. Being crammed in a car with a stranger for hours could take away from the journey. The same can be said about reading a book by an author you do not know very well. Books can be very personal and meaningful, but this sentiment can be lost in the anonymity or secrecy of the author. This is why I want to invite you to get a glimpse of my personal life, in the hope it will help this book come to life for both you and me.

I know what you might be thinking, *"What kind of author waits until chapter five to properly introduce himself to the reader?"* Well, you will soon find out that I certainly do not love being the center of attention, especially when it comes to talking about myself. However, for the words of the other storytellers to resonate in your heart, you must understand why they first meant something special to me.

Each story, following my own, will share a lesson that has helped me in my life in one aspect or another. After reading my story and learning about the path I have been walking, you will be able to see a glimmer of me in each story that follows. I hope that you see not only me but also yourself in at least one of the stories you are about to read. If I was able to find strength and support in the words of the others in this book, I sincerely think you can too.

Buckle up, get comfy, and prepare yourself to learn much more about the person who put these words on this page: Me!

Welcome to *the Mile Behind my Smile.*

* * *

On a hot, yet windy, May Sunday morning, I heard the cheers of my friends and family as I walked across the stage to receive my college diploma.

For many, this monumental, ten-second walk, represents a significant change in the direction of their lives. With the handing of the diploma and the moving of the tassel, the life you lived as a college student is instantaneously replaced with the starting of a career. With dreams of law school, doing a year of faith-led service in Jamaica or Ecuador, working at one of the biggest accounting firms in Ohio, or so many more dream jobs, this moment brings excellent momentum into the next stage of our lives.

However, as my name was called and my feet drug across the stage, my mind was filled with many different thoughts. In the crowd to my left was a sea of familiar faces. As my eyes scanned across them, memories would flash in and out of my head. This moment was similar to how people often say your life flashes before your eyes right before you are going to die. In my case, the person I had grown to become in college was the one vanishing as I received my diploma and smiled for the cameras.

However, nobody was actually dying as I ventured across the stage, that is just something my mind loves to do: over-analyze every interaction, scenario, and conversation that I experience throughout the course of my day. Overthinking and worrying are two of my most common hobbies, so it came as no surprise that my mind was racing even on such a celebratory day. However, I could not help myself; I did not want to lose the life I had developed on this college campus.

For me, the time spent at college was much more than sitting in a classroom for four years to prepare me to work hard for the next forty. I decided to attend a college where I would know not a single soul in an attempt to seek something much more significant than wisdom: happiness.

* * *

If you asked people in my life to tell you a bit about me, the answers might include some of these buzzwords: "sweet," "kind," and "happy." In other words, I am the friendly kid with a smile on his face and funny socks on his feet. If you ever need someone to laugh at any joke you make, no matter how bad it is, I am your guy. The smallest of things can cause a smile to spread across my face, likely due to still being a child at heart and finding fascination in many things. That said, I try my best to be the one thinking positively, even in tough situations, like booking the wrong flight or when there may be drama engulfing a group of friends.

I like to view the world with a "glass-half-full" lens. Whenever I would catch myself feeling bad for me, I would quickly remind myself that there are others in the world suffering more than I and that I should not dwell on things that may upset me for too long. However, that does not explain why I would be seeking happiness at college.

* * *

Growing up, I was raised in a family who gave me more love than I could have ever imagined. My mother has the kindest heart and willingness to help me with anything, and my father offering endless advice when it came to my indecisiveness and insecurities. I have two older brothers who stood up for me and a younger sister whom I have been figuratively attached to since the day she came home from the hospital. However, this affection given to me was not met with love I would, in turn, give myself.

I was, and often still am, the world's harshest critic when it came to myself, dwelling on every small mistake and turning molehills into mountains that stood in the way of my happiness. The kindness I would show others was never shown to myself, but I would never let this part of my life show to anyone else. I often hear remarks such as "I have never seen Cal mad at anyone before," but what people did not know was that I was too busy being upset with myself to worry about others.

At an early age, I developed several speech impediments that turned the bubbly child I once was into a timid boy, scared of opening his mouth in fear of embarrassment. I still remember the day in my elementary school classroom when I had the realization that my speech was underdeveloped.

I would always love to raise my hand and answer questions, showing my teacher that I genuinely enjoyed being in school. So when my teacher asked if anyone would like to read part of a book out loud, my hand naturally was the first to shoot up. As I began reading out loud at my desk, my mind focused on being able to read each word, but my concentration was soon disrupted by giggling. I tried to continue reading, but I kept asking myself why other kids were laughing, the last sentence I said could not have been THAT funny. In that moment, I knew they were laughing at me. I finished the last sentence with a wobbly voice, ashamed of myself for not speaking perfectly.

I went from eagerly talking to friends and participating in class to forcing myself not to speak to avoid being mocked or being asked, "Why do you talk like that?" day after day. With each interaction I would have, I felt the pressure of judgment from my peers weighing heavily on my shoulders. My parents watched the joy and excitement I once had for school slowly fade from within me. What was left was a boy too afraid even to raise his hand in class to go to the bathroom in fear of feeling the twenty sets of eyes in the classroom looking at me, judging me.

As I grew older, the sneering comments from those around me had slowly fizzled out, but I was still always faced with my biggest bully: myself. I associated social interaction with humiliation, which developed into a fear of meeting new people, speaking in class, and just talking in general. Throughout high school, I felt myself finding the comfort of hiding in the shadows of my two brothers. As they became their own unique selves through athletics and academics, I found security in simply being known as the youngest of the Long triplets.

By blending in with the background, I gave up my happiness and self-identity to put my anxiety at ease, thinking people will have to like me if they like my brothers. At the end of the day, the person I was pretending to be was not authentic, but rather an attempt to avoid the pain of humiliation.

By choosing to attend college away from the comfort of familiarity, I was taking a risk to find happiness. Finding the opportunity to start fresh, apart from the history of hiding and fearing judgment, was a blessing in disguise. Each day I challenged myself to speak to someone new and to fight the feeling of hiding how I talk. I told myself that if I wanted to be happy, I had to stop constraining myself in every conversation I have.

Over the next four years, I would cross paths with countless people who have made such a dramatic impact on my life; some are even included in this book. I found people that would lift me up rather than allowing me to push myself down. Through each meaningful and heartfelt friendship, I learned that imperfections are not inadequacies, but rather opportunities to let others into your life to help you heal. Through their constant support, I found myself in opportunities I would have never expected, such as:

→ Hosting an award show in London for the other thirty-four other students
→ Participating in a team to put together a retreat for fifty-five other retreatants
→ Being an emcee for a Dance Marathon with over 200 attendees

My happiness was no longer found in hiding, but rather accepting myself for who I have always been.

* * *

The funny thing is that the aspect of my life, the way I talk, that has dictated and constrained me mentally and metaphorically is just one small characteristic about me. As I have discussed this with others, they are quick to tell me that they do not even notice anything when I talk. Instead, it is just a small part of me that makes me unique. How could people not notice something that I think about every time I open my mouth? The fact of the matter is that sometimes an issue is only as big as you make it. You can blow something out of proportion, allowing it to leave a lasting impact, when, in reality, others barely even notice. I have learned that your **insecurities only have as much power over you as you give them**, showing your confidence in yourself diminishes the impact they will end up having on you.

However, this does not mean that I am entirely "fixed." There are still many days where I feel my heart pounding and my head spinning as if there is a tornado within whenever I have to speak up. There are days when I pick apart every single word I said in a conversation, criticizing myself until I lie in bed at night. Moments still exist when I feel paralyzed with doubt, feeling all the confidence from within seeping out of me.

However, that does not stop me from approaching each new day with a smile on my face. What is different between these feelings now and how I previously experienced them years ago is how I react to them. Rather than letting them dictate my life, forcing me into a lifestyle of hiding and limiting myself, I choose to forgive myself and forget. If the people around me do not care about how I talk, which is what caused the constant fear and anxious feelings in the start, why should I care?

A question I often ask myself is, "*If you treated and talked to others the way you treat/talk to yourself, how would they feel?*" Although it may be a silly question to ask, it helps me realize that I would never want to treat others the way I once treated myself. The constant criticism and pressure I put on myself would be such a burden for me to place on others, so why do I continue to treat myself this way? It is so natural and easy for us to be quick to judge ourselves for not being "normal," yet we would rarely ever treat others the same way. The love and support we show to others must also be shown to ourselves to be healthy and happy truly.

* * *

In complete honesty, this chapter is one of the first times I have ever spoken about this part of my life, however I wanted to stay true to my message of telling our stories. It also gives you a look into my world and why I would be inclined to write a book on this topic. I may not have an education in counseling or psychology, but I know what it feels like to need someone's guidance and support, to be lost and feeling defeated. However, I also know what it feels like to learn of someone's story and become connected to their words and their journey. As my ears are flooded with their pain and vulnerability, I have become more comfortable with myself, knowing that I am not the only one who has had rough patches in life. It is a strange concept, to struggle together in unity, but it is comforting to know that someone you may look up to has been through a similar or even tougher battle, and they have been able to overcome.

If they can fight each day and climb their mountain, so can you.

Reflection

Please take this time to find a comfortable position to sit and quiet your mind. Let my story resonate in your heart as you reflect on the following questions:

1. What is one thing about you that you find yourself often criticizing?

2. What are three things about you of which you are proud?

3. How can you remind yourself to go easier on yourself and recognize the good inside you?

Song for Reflection: "Got It In You" (Acoustic) by BANNERS

Chapter 6:
Mollie

"You will find that it is necessary to let things go; simply for the reason that they are heavy."

—C JOYBELL C.

Everyone you meet has a story unique to them. From start to finish, no two people have the same life path, making our stories unique and essential. As books fill the shelves of a library, billions of people with their own stories fill the world in which we live. At first glance, you might think you know what a book is about from the cover, but there is always so much more to a person than what first meets the eye.

This idea of not judging a book by its cover brings me to my friend, Mollie. We first met when we studied together in London for a semester during our sophomore year in college. She first introduced herself to me at a bar where I was clearly out of my element. Despite a large group of our classmates being together, I was still in the early stages of getting to know everyone, and my shyness was getting the best of me that night. Out of the thirty-four students who came from our home university, I could count the number of people I knew on one hand.

On this particular night, I was near the outskirts of our group, not really interacting with those around me. As the music blared over the speakers and strangers danced around me, my eyes frantically scanned the room, looking for a familiar face. My heart began beating faster in my chest, with each moment passing of not feeling at ease and wishing I could be at home. Despite the feeling of discomfort growing inside me, I wore a smile on my face trying to fit in with everyone else. That is when Mollie approached me and introduced herself. She smiled at me, shook my hand in the middle of a crowded room, and said,

"Hi, my name is Mollie, my mom used to not drink in college either, so I think it is so cool that you do not drink."

Throughout the night, she would occasionally ask how I was doing, and if I was having fun. Each interaction was serving as a reminder to me that I was not alone. This small moment and kind face among the sea of unfamiliarity has had a lasting impact on me.

Fast forward to the present day, and Mollie is still the happy, loving person she was almost three years ago. Despite having a schedule busy with work, soccer, and a double major, she never fails to help those around her. One of her most memorable experiences is participating in a Friday-night service activity of delivering food and clothing to the less fortunate. Growing up near the Cleveland area, it was eye-opening to see how many people in her community are suffering and being marginalized.

One man that she met while delivering food, which we will keep anonymous, has always been in the back of her mind. He lives outside of the Cleveland Browns' stadium, and she sees his living spaces set up occasionally as she drives downtown. To many, this stadium is a source of entertainment to watch a football game for a few hours and forget the problems they may be facing at home. However, for him, this stadium was his home; there was no escape from his reality. Despite this, he approached life with a positive attitude that many of us lack. His kindness and appreciation toward Mollie showed her that even when you might not expect it, you can find love in the hearts of strangers.

Mollie's love for serving others stems from her growing up in a Catholic school environment where her faith would become a large part of her life. Like many teenagers, she struggled to connect with the Catholic teachings in a classroom setting. Rather than sitting at a desk, she was able to find a connection with her God while engaging in service. Through service, rather than viewing God in a scary light who punishes those who sin, Mollie began seeing God as a loving being. She recognized God's love in the people she met and the stories they shared. Much like the man outside the Cleveland Browns' stadium, everybody has a lesson to share. That is why we are all placed on this Earth. God has a plan for all of us, and the only way for us to understand this is to hear the stories of others.

Before carrying on with the rest of Mollie's story, I would like you to think about the details shared about her. From just a brief glance into her life, you may feel that you can create a fair idea of her in your mind. However, a book is more than just the first few pages, and a person is more than just first impressions.

* * *

Behind Mollie's loving and comforting personality hides a girl who has struggled with anxiety and depression for ten years. During this part of her life, she could not get out of her bed, was not eating, and even wanted to end her own life. The decade of letting anxiety weigh her down to the depths of the ocean had finally consumed her. During the darkest time in her life, she refused to get help from anyone: friends, family, or even professionals. She did not want to burden anyone with her problems and kept them all to herself, only making the scars deeper. Looking back on these times, Mollie recalled that,

> "The only time I felt truly at peace was when I was asleep. I started thinking about what it would be like to sleep forever, all the worrying and pain would be gone. Nobody would even miss me since I was just miserable anyway."

Each day was getting darker and darker, her worrying only worsened.

During these times, she was selected to be a participant on a student-led spiritual retreat at her university called Manresa. It is named after Manresa, Spain, one of the places where Saint Ignatius stopped on his journey to reflect significantly on "his life, his limitations, and his love for God."[18] This is exactly what the retreat offered to the students who attended, a weekend away from the stress of school to reflect on faith and life.

Another component of the retreat is allowing several student leaders to give a talk about Ignatius' Spirituality and how it has helped guide their lives. Through these talks, students portray significant vulnerability in sharing their stories, not hiding any detail about personal struggles they have experienced and how they have persevered. The first talk is about finding God, or love, in all things. This talk is the one that changed the course of Mollie's life. The student who gave this talk taught Mollie and the rest of the students that there is no shame about getting help from other people. The student expressed great vulnerability and openness, showing everyone that they are not alone in their personal struggles; everyone is struggling with their own internal battle in one way or another.

To Mollie, that weekend was a turning point. It led her to the true purpose of why God had placed her in the lives

18   "Manresa Retreat." Campus Ministry. John Carroll University.

of others: *to tell her story.* She decided to finally reach out and get help from a therapist who continually improved Mollie's life by allowing her to discuss her anxious thoughts openly. Through this, she became comfortable letting out her feelings and not bottling them up, even if it was just to a therapist.

As time progressed, she was given the opportunity to help lead the same retreat that created such a positive impact in her life. While applying, she wanted to give the same talk, Talk One, because she knew how big an impact it had made on her life just several months prior. However, nobody else in her personal life truly knew what she was going through; her battle was internal. Giving a talk in front of fifty students about how she has immensely suffered from anxiety to the point she wanted to end her life would be the first time she had ever publicly spoken about her mental health. She was self-conscious about the idea that people would know of her deepest darkest secret. However, her mom told her the advice that would make everything worth it:

"If you talk about all of this and even just one person resonates with it, it is worth it. If anyone relates to even just one part of what you say and it helps them, it is worth it."

In this moment, everything became much clearer. Mollie was not given her depression or anxiety as a punishment in life, but rather so she could overcome this obstacle and share her story to inspire those who also suffer. Her life was saved from someone being vulnerable with their story with her, and now it was her turn to continue the favor. Mollie knew that if she wanted to be truly happy, she had to be open about her heavy past. She wanted to prove to herself that she is not weighed down by it anymore, but instead, she is in control.

Months after giving the talk, Mollie had a new appreciation of the love in life. Through the retreat and allowing herself to be vulnerable and share her story, she has found great happiness and love from those around her. In life, it is far easier to question why something wrong is happening rather than wondering how you can grow from the opportunity. There comes great strength and wisdom as you overcome any obstacle that stands in your way, no matter the size. From not allowing her depression and anxiety to weigh her down as much, Mollie is able to live a much happier and freeing life. The thoughts that would cloud her head with negativity have faded, allowing the sun to shine and radiate warmth.

* * *

Before I had learned of Mollie's past, I only knew her as the popular soccer girl who seemed to have everything going for her in her life. I knew she was beloved around campus, and I thought she had a perfect life, but I too only read her first few pages. When we first met, I was allowing my anxiety to get the best of me due to new surroundings, new people, and a new country that made me completely overwhelmed. Perhaps she recognized this in me and knew that I could use a friend, after struggling with anxiety herself for so long.

I first learned of Mollie's battle with anxiety when she joined Jamie's Work in Progress campaign around campus that featured students discussing their mental health issues and how they combat them. Upon this discovery, I was utterly shocked and disappointed at my ignorance. How could this happy, loving girl who took the time to get to know me when I was facing anxiety be experiencing a similar obstacle?

Mollie taught me that *anyone in your life could be struggling with a battle that you would never expect*, which is why it is so important to tell people that they are not alone. I want to be someone's Mollie: I want to help showcase that even the happiest of people have been through tough times, but life does get better.

Finding comfort in other people helps you **leave the heavy past behind** and live the rest of your life with your full happiness. I may have been fated to stumble upon this lesson from one of my close friends, or it could just be one of the many examples that exist in the world. There are people like Mollie who will share their story to help others around the world, in every community, and everyone's life. All it takes is having the courage to speak up and impact even one person. Who knows, the person you impact might even decide to write a book based on a lesson you taught them.

* * *

It is important to understand the differences between general unhappiness and feelings of depression. People mistake their sadness and often self-diagnose themselves with depression, while others who do suffer from depression may treat it as just sadness, fearing the word "depression." After asking counselors at my university and researching online, I have learned that sadness can be felt about a certain thing, such as denting your car, doing poorly on an exam, or losing something of sentimental value. As time passes, so does this feeling.

Depression, on the other hand, does not fade. Rather than being upset about something, you feel sad about everything; nothing will lift your spirits, not even time. *Psychology Today* describes depression as a cloud that "covers all aspects of our lives, making everything less enjoyable, less interesting, less important, less lovable, and less worthwhile. Depression saps our energy, motivation, and ability to experience joy, pleasure, excitement, anticipation, satisfaction, connection, and meaning."[19]

However, this does not mean that sadness is just a phase that will run its course with time like a common cold. Feeling unhappy is one of the symptoms of developing depression, especially if it is consistent. Prolonged sadness can create the feeling of numbness to emotional pain, and the enjoyment of

---

19 Winch, Guy. "The Important Difference Between Sadness and Depression." *Psychology Today*. Sussex Publishers, October 2, 2015

life will fade. Those who suffer from depression tend to hide their pain, while it may be easier to recognize when someone is unhappy due to their actions, words, or expressions.

Regardless, people who may be showing signs of either should be treated with care, shown love, and taken seriously. Check on your friends. Even the kindest, like Mollie, may be hiding something deep inside.

For resources regarding anxiety & depression, please visit the following organizations' websites:

Mental Health America

Anxiety and Depression Association of America

Or call 1-800-273-8255.

You are not alone.

Reflection

Please take this time to find a comfortable position to sit in and quiet your mind. Let Mollie's story resonate in your heart and reflect on the following questions.

1. What is something that is heavy on your heart or mind right now?

2. What is your story to tell?

3. How can you be someone's Mollie?

Song for Reflection: "Heavy" by Birdtalker

Chapter 7:
Fabienne

"Happiness blooms from within"

A common phrase used to describe searching for happiness in life is "finding the light at the end of the tunnel." In this sentence, it infers that you are on a path of complete darkness, both physically and metaphorically. Put yourself in this mentality for a moment, in a dark, dark tunnel. Your surroundings are bleak. The tunnel is cold, with cement walls that confine you to the path that you are forced to walk. Your eyes scan your surroundings frantically, searching for even a glimpse of light. Then you see it — the distant light at the end of the tunnel. How far away are you from this light? Are you just a few steps, or do miles stand between you and this source of light or happiness?

For many who find themselves walking this lonely path, they often feel the latter of the two, the light being miles away. What this expression tells us is that even though you see a murmur of happiness at the end, you still could have a long journey of darkness until you reach the light. This promotes the idea that suffering now will be worth it once you reach the happiness, no matter how treacherous a walk it may be. However, why must we accept the state of suffering?

Emotional healing therapist Fabienne rebutted these common words of encouragement with some wisdom of her own, saying,

> "Stop trying to reach for the happiness at the end of the tunnel and start finding the happiness inside you. Rather than accepting the darkness, find the happiness and joy in every single moment of life, and that light at the end of the tunnel is not so distant."

Throughout her life, Fabienne has learned that **happiness indeed does reside in all of us.** It is not something we have to achieve, but rather something we rediscover from within us.

Like many of us, Fabienne had to learn this lesson the hard way. At the age of forty-four, Fabienne received a phone call that devastated her and made her question the world in which she was living. The call was from her husband, who she had happily been married to for twenty years. What she thought was just a routine phone call with the man she loved turned out to be something quite the opposite. He wanted a divorce.

At this moment, Fabienne felt as if her life had just hit "restart." Everything she had known and grown to love in the past twenty years was all taken away from her with just the four words, "I want a divorce."

These four words continued to haunt her as she felt her heart continue to shatter. Like a baseball through a windshield, the spiderweb cracks too deep to be repaired. She went to therapists seeking happiness through their words and healing. As she sat in the chair facing her therapist, she realized that happiness is not a gift that can just be given from one person to another. No matter the pills she swallowed or the hours she spent telling her story, her heart did not heal. In the three months following, she attempted to take her own life twice, giving up on her search for happiness. She found herself in a deep, dark tunnel, but there was no light to be seen.

Fabienne found her solution through meeting with a therapist who specialized in hypnotherapy and life counseling. Through each session she had with him, she found comfort in hearing him say, "I am here for you, do not worry." Having these weekly interactions with him gave her something to look forward to each week, giving her the strength to fight through the pain of daily obligations to have it all relieved. Having another human voice tell her that she matters helped her realize her purpose in life. She wanted to be that voice for others who are struggling. When asked what exactly she meant by her purpose, Fabienne told me that she does not want anyone to be on this journey alone or wandering down the wrong path.

Fabienne now works as an emotional healing therapist, where she has been able to be the voice of love to hundreds of unique individuals. What she has learned from hearing so many stories of agony, pain, and struggling is that no two people require the same exact treatment. Whether it is helping women overcome a divorce like her or helping a struggling teen get out of bed each morning, she understands that people of all ages, gender, and background are suffering. Although two people may be suffering from a similar disorder, trauma, or problem, it does not mean that they require the same attention. Everyone's story and history are unique to them, meaning there is not a universal relief such as a painkiller for a headache. This may be frustrating to those who desire a quick fix, but what will help the healing comes from within you, not someone or something else.

When she first started her counseling career, most of her clients were primarily middle-aged women because they felt comfortable speaking to a counselor who was like them. There is comfort in familiarity, but sometimes going outside of this comfort zone is where people tend to find their solutions. In recent years, she has been helping younger people in their early twenties, both men and women. Societal values have been continuously changing, which reflects the changing of her clientele. The pressures of being perfect, both their online personas and living up to expectations set by society, are weighing heavier and heavier on younger people these days. While social media demands them to appear flawless, society expects them to be successful and ready to make an impact in the world right out of college. This dilemma then causes a sense of not knowing who they truly are and who they want to be.

Despite these changing pressures on both men and women, there is one positive trend about society — people are more willing to ask for help. People are becoming less hesitant to seek advice to rediscover their happiness, especially those in the younger generation. Each year, she helps more and more young people. This is not to say that the current generation is suffering more than those before, but instead, they view it as more acceptable to seek help.

In the past, attending therapy would be kept a secret, in fear of what others may think of you when they find out. Sharing with others that you attend therapy might raise concern, causing others to question your mental state and stability. Whereas today, it has become much more normalized to be open about seeking help, rather than hiding this part of your life. Telling others that it is okay to seek help not only helps diminish the stigma but could open the door for them to become interested in seeking therapy as well.

However, Fabienne does not view her job as providing the solution to her clients or helping move them along to find the light at the end of their tunnel. She believes that the light has always been inside of them, but sometimes they just need some help to realize this. Every day, she pushes herself to help others reconnect with their inner happiness.

"Most babies are born happy, despite all the crying that comes with being born," Fabienne reminded me, to emphasize that everyone is born with happiness inside of them. However, this happiness can be pushed deep down, overshadowed by the chaos that comes in life. Rather than fighting each day to become one step closer to the end of a tunnel, Fabienne urges people to look inside their hearts and minds to rediscover their happiness.

Reflecting on the journey of her life and all the ups and downs, Fabienne feels at peace. She gets reminded each day of the happiness inside of her as she helps others search for their own. To her, happiness is *"enjoying the great moments in life, and not being afraid when you cannot find them."* In other words, to feel true happiness, it cannot be just a fleeting emotion in life that can change in an instant. However, it is a state of mind, where even when we have a bad day, we can recognize all the good that may have happened.

Happiness is not just a light at the end of a long, lonely tunnel or something you achieve after checking off items on a bucket list. Although there will be days where it is harder to believe there is a reason to be happy truly, have faith. **Happiness is inside all of us, no matter how bleak life may be at the moment.**

There is happiness inside of each and every one of us, I promise.

Reflection

Please take this time to find a comfortable position to sit in and quiet your mind. Let Fabienne's story resonate in your heart and reflect on the following questions.

1. Who are three people you would tell "I am here for you, do not worry"?

2. How can you remind these people that you are there for them?

3. What are ways you can remind yourself of the happiness you have within you?

Song for Reflection: "Be Still" by the Fray

Chapter 8:
Gianna

**"I can do all things through Christ
who strengthens me"**

—Philippians 4:13

In life, everyone around you is being weighed down by their own unique anchor. They come in all shapes and sizes, personally tailored to the person to which they are attached. Although it may not appear so, the people you walk past in the streets likely have something on their mind that is bringing down their mood and adding extra weight on their shoulders.

Whether it is stress from work, a troubled relationship, insecurities, or a blend of different factors of life, an anchor can cause significant strain on the happiness in life. The heavier a topic gets, the more it becomes a negative force in someone's life. Although the anchor is just within someone's mind, it can still create the feeling of dragging an actual anchor everywhere they go. No matter what they do, this anchor will be weighing on their mind, pushing them to their physical limits. There are days where many find the strength to carry this extra weight flawlessly, but then there are instances where the anchor wins and prevents future growth and happiness.

However, an "anchor" in life can be used in a much different, more positive way. Another way to look at an anchor is in the metaphorical form of "being someone's anchor." Rather than being something weighing down a boat, an anchor can be used to keep something, or someone, stable. Whether it is through comfort, emotional support, or just being there for someone else, becoming an anchor is a task everyone can accomplish.

Despite the difference in meanings, both forms of anchors can be related. As humans, we can take what is weighing us down and grow from it, so much so that we can spread our message to those around us. We gain strength in picking our anchors up, enough to become a support system for those who need it. Although we may have previously been weighed down, our anchors allow us to grow stronger, eventually strong enough to overcome them.

This leads to the story of Gianna, a woman who truly turned the meaning of an anchor around throughout the course of her life. Gianna's journey of redefining her anchor stems back to her early childhood, where she was fighting battles even back then.

When thinking back to elementary school, many of us view it as a time when things were much easier and the biggest problems we faced were learning how to tie our shoes or spelling basic words. Elementary schools create a sense of fun and excitement while children are away from home for eight hours of the day. However, in second grade, Gianna was faced with an anchor that she could not avoid: Gym Class.

The time dedicated throughout the week for kids to run off all their extra energy created more fear than benefits for Gianna. Each day she had gym class, she recalls an intense feeling of dread overcoming her, she just truly hated it. Every car ride to school consisted of her continually begging for her mother to write her a note to excuse her from that class. No matter what was going on in her life, the idea of gym class always filled her with fear.

Like all good moms, Gianna's mother gave her some advice to help her survive the day and give her the strength she needed at the time, even if it is strength to survive just gym class. During one of the car rides early in the morning, Gianna's mother told her to repeat this phrase in her head over and over whenever she felt scared, this phrase being "I can do all things through Christ who strengthens me." Gianna recalls that her mother has always shown her unconditional love and radiated positivity, so if she could keep this quote always in her mind, maybe she could be the same way. Sure enough, the terror that came with gym class slowly began to fade as Gianna realized the strength that she had inside of her.

An important detail to note is that Gianna often references God as the source of her strength, which may not be as meaningful to those who do not follow any particular faith or religion. However, she describes God as "love" and that the two can be used interchangeably. In other words, when she talks about her God, she can also be talking about the love that exists around her. "God" has a different meaning to every person, and I urge you to replace this word with whatever fits best with your faith and with what you are most comfortable.

As Gianna continued her life, she soon would face an obstacle that left a deeper scar than simply fearing gym class. In middle school, Gianna began to see herself differently, thinking that she would be happier if she were prettier and lost weight.

When talking about this part of her life, Gianna mentions how she "had a goal of what I wanted to weigh and told myself I would stop dieting once I got to that point. However, that point came, and I made a new, lower goal for myself, ...and then another, and another. I felt like I was accomplishing something and got a surge of joy every time I saw that number on the scale drop. It became an obsession."

She was in a downward spiral, her mindset on being happier through losing more and more weight. Except no matter what she lost, she was not pleased. It took a visit to a doctor for her to understand what was causing her to slip into this mindset; she had developed anorexia nervosa.

For the next eight and a half years of her life, Gianna was fighting her urge not to eat and feel numb to her emotions. By not eating, she allowed herself not to have enough energy to focus on how she felt. However, it also caused her to feel the "life draining out of her bones, physically, emotionally, and spiritually." Despite her history of seeking help from different types of treatment centers, dietitians, and therapists, she never felt the strength to open up about it, not even to her closest friends. She was suffering silently from her disorder, searching for the strength to overcome.

Gianna would continue praying for strength. As time passed, she was slowly building up the power to carry her anchor, trying to overcome her eating disorder fully. However, no matter how hard she would try, there was still always a small piece of the anchor still weighing on her heart, keeping her from being happy. During her second year in college, Gianna realized that she had to change the way she was thinking. To do so, she needed to gain strength from those around her and not entirely depend on herself to overcome an anchor that has been weighing her down for eight grueling years.

Like Mollie's story, she was given the opportunity to talk about her journey to an open group of students, which would allow her to release everything she had been holding in for years finally. However, this opportunity scared her beyond belief. She did not want to open up about such a vulnerable time in her life. If she was not able to talk to even her closest of friends in high school, why would she tell a large group of strangers? While she continuously would go back and forth on this opportunity, a song came on the radio as she was driving her car, and she felt the switch flip in her head. The song "Your Hands" by JJ Heller flooded the car with the message that she had been waiting to hear.

The lyrics echoed the quote her mother told her to always say in her head when she needed strength before gym class. To her, the song is a reminder that "even in tough times when my heart is breaking, I will never be alone. God is with me through everything, even if I cannot see it." Hearing these lyrics and understanding that the strength she gets from God and her loved ones around her, Gianna was finally able to let go of the last part of her past that was once so heavy. She found the support and strength she had been searching for from her friends, family, and faith, after eight long years of trying to face this on her own.

* * *

This change in perspective allowed Gianna to live her life the way she was destined to fully. She gained her happiness from making those around her smile. By radiating the love that she learned from her mother, she makes all those around her feel at home in her presence. As soon as Gianna begins talking to someone, she utters her words with such a kindness that every conversation brighten someone's day. She attributes her loving personality to the journey she has been through and discovering the love that always existed within her.

Having dealt with struggling to love herself for so many years, Gianna does not want anyone else to feel the way she once did, silently fighting a battle by refusing to let others into this side of her life. Through every warm interaction, every wave, and smile she gives as she walks the sidewalks of her campus, she is offering her support to every familiar face to help lift their anchors.

By becoming a source of support to those around her, Gianna exemplifies the concept of being a source of positivity that helps boost her happiness as well. As she continues to be a beacon of light for all, she finds herself much happier than when she numbed her thoughts and emotions. In a study done by Barbara Fredrickson, it is argued that positive emotions not only impact the people around us and us temporarily but can create a lasting impact in the long term.[20] The study also creates an "important prescriptive message. People should cultivate positive emotions in their own lives and the lives of those around them, not just because doing so makes them feel good in the moment, but also because doing so transforms people for the better and sets them on paths toward flourishing."[21]

There will be times when positivity is hard to find, and when the thoughts inside your head are the complete opposite. Whether it is thinking negatively about fears as small as gym class, or as massive as thoughts about yourself, it can control your life. One negative thought leads to another, creating a

---

20 Fredrickson, Barbara. "The Broaden-and-Build Theory of Positive Emotions." The Royal Society. University of Michigan, August 17, 2004.
21 Ibid.

patterned routine until it is too late: the negativity in your head has consumed your entire view on life, the anchor dragging you down.

However, **it is never too late to turn this mindset around.** You could be fighting over eight years with the negative thoughts inside your head and still come out a survivor, like Gianna. As she has grown over the years, her positivity toward herself and those around her has allowed her to truly blossom and flourish. All it takes is deciding that today is the day you turn things around. Day by day, we can determine if we want to react positively or negatively to situations. We decide if we want to be dragged down or be challenged to carry on. Is this anchor going to continue weighing you down, or is it an opportunity for growth?

The decision is yours.

Reflection

Please take this time to find a comfortable position to sit in and quiet your mind. Let Gianna's story resonate in your heart and reflect on the following questions.

1. What is an anchor that has weighed you down in the past?

2. What are three ways you can be an anchor to support someone else?

3. Who are three people who have been an anchor for you?

Song for Reflection: "Your Hands" by JJ Heller

Chapter 9:
Erin

———

"When the roots are deep, there is
no reason to fear the wind"

—AFRICAN PROVERB

Throughout our lives, we are continually changing and growing, both physically and emotionally. This growth that we are constantly undergoing is like that of a tree. Even the tallest of trees that stand high above our heads came from nothing but roots. A tree would not be able to stand firmly in its place if it were not for the roots offering support.

As humans, we cannot grow without firmly establishing our roots as well. Unlike trees, we, fortunately, do not have roots growing out of us to keep us in place, but rather our roots are metaphoric. We cannot grow as human beings without understanding who we truly are. The song "Roots Before Branches" expresses this idea through the lyrics, which I invite you to listen to at the end of this chapter.

This song was first brought to my attention from a woman named Erin, who first heard the song on an episode of *Glee*. As she continued to listen to the repetition of the lyrics, she felt them begin to resonate more and more with her current lifestyle and changes she was facing. As she listened to the song on repeat during a flight, she began to think about her life in great detail.

Erin was once just a typical high school student in the lovely state of Idaho. She grew up in a small town where everyone seemed to have the same "rub some dirt on it" attitude toward pain. With her father raised as a farmer, her entire family was shaped around having a tough mentality and not showing physical evidence of pain or weakness. Being raised in this environment shaped her personality into being tough and not letting her emotions show, for she feared being seen as weak.

By the time she was in high school, Erin had found herself surrounded by the different cliques and felt the need to conform to one of them to fit in. Looking around the cafeteria, she could see all the "jocks," "cheerleaders," and "cool kids" and felt the need to compare herself to all of them and wonder how she could fit in with them. Erin was a multi-sport athlete, so she was able to form friendships with the athletes that she would spend countless hours with during practice and games. However, she felt that through this lifestyle she was living, the tough athlete, she was not her true authentic self.

When it came time to apply to colleges, she reflected on the life she had been living. At the time, she was reading the book *A Portrait of the Artist as a Young Man* by James Joyce. This book revolves around the life of Stephen Dedalus, an Irish boy growing up near the end of the nineteenth century.[22] Throughout the course of the book, he finds himself gradually casting out all the constraints he feels in his life. He lets go of his social, religious, and family limitations to devote his life to the art of writing. The book follows his life as he decides to attend university away from his family to pursue his passions.[23]

While reading the book, the message of discovering what the heart is and what the heart wants away from the familiarity of friends and family could not escape Erin's mind. At this point in her life, Erin had created a comfortable lifestyle for herself. She was able to find friends through her athletics, her church, and her small town. However, she was not satisfied with the life she was so familiar with; she wanted to let her roots expand and be able to grow as her own person, not the person she was shaped out to be in Idaho. And with that, she decided to attend school in Ohio, nearly 2,000 miles from the comfort of her home and her inauthentic identity.

As Erin entered into this new chapter of her story, fear was always on her mind, not knowing what would come next or if she was doing the right thing for herself. By going to college in Ohio, she was not only losing the safety of her friends and family, but she also was losing everything she was known for

---

22 Joyce, James. *Dubliners; A Portrait of the Artist as a Young Man.* New York: Barnes & Noble, 1992.

23 Ibid.

in high school. At her college, Erin was the only student from Idaho, the only Mormon, and she went from playing two sports in high school to playing none. She lost the comfort of knowing all the other students, members of her church, and her teammates, creating some internal struggles for her.

Unlike students who go to a college somewhat close to home, Erin was not a short drive away from her parents; she had isolated herself in Ohio. To make matters worse for her, she began to second-guess her decision to major in nursing, which she thought would be a safe major for her. With all these negative thoughts and emotions piling up, Erin questioned if she made the right decision to branch out and try to find her true identity.

After spending the first semester in Ohio, Erin knew that she, once again, had to make a change in her life if she wanted to be happy. She decided to attend a college far from home, and she was not going to give up on it just yet. The following semester, she decided to join a sorority and become heavily involved in Greek life. It was this decision where she felt herself beginning to feel at peace with the life she has been living. As she entered into this new community of women within the campus, she felt true unity. Rather than facing these unfamiliar faces with fear, she was welcomed by them, and she finally found the home for which she was searching.

As she grew older, Erin developed a passion for creating programs for Greek life revolving around providing support to others. She wanted to give back to the organization that helped her roots grow and support her as she continued throughout college. All the programs she created revolved around the word "*story*," and she always emphasized the idea of being proud of the story your life is writing, which can be hard. While in college, she noticed that a lot of the women around her would fall into the mindset of self-comparison through social media, a topic discussed earlier in this book. This unhappiness will dampen and damage the identity you are creating for yourself, making you think that your story is not the best it could be.

By seeing this struggle inside people, Erin became passionate about helping them. Erin decided to abandon the tough personality she was raised to have in Idaho and become vulnerable to these women, discussing her struggles with loneliness the prior semester. In doing this, Erin wanted to create an environment for the other girls to feel welcomed and supported in opening up about their own battles as well. Many people who struggle with mental health tend to bottle it up inside them, letting the toxicity spread from head to toe rather than releasing it out. By opening up and letting go of the idea that you should only know your struggles, you feel a sense of strength that is like no other feeling. You are no longer confined to the small pot you were put in, but rather your roots can finally grow.

No matter how bleak and dark your past may have been, it still serves as part of your story. Everything you have been through matters to you. **Every experience you have had in**

your life strengthens your roots, allowing you to grow. Through our many life experiences, we can learn what we love to do and what we do not love doing. Even an adverse event in your life proves to you that you can overcome that obstacle and likely any others that come your way. With this mentality, you can reflect and see how you have been shaped from each experience. As you continue growing into your authentic identity, you will be much happier than you ever would have been pretending to be somebody you are not.

To Erin, happiness is "when you can look around and see how your past has connected you to your future, that every decision you have made and action you have done lines up and allows your future to fall into place." Through all of Erin's story, she has struggled with finding her identity for years and had to take extreme steps to try to find out who she truly is. By becoming involved in Greek life and helping all of those in her community, she discovered her love for helping others through tough times. If it were not for her risk of moving to Ohio and extending her roots, she might have never found her identity. As her roots became planted, she continued to grow and blossom. She soon realized that she wanted to study counseling psychology, which she is currently working on now. Erin told me that "after learning so much from the programs I created to help others be proud of their story and tracing back my journey, I knew I could see myself doing this for years."

* * *

In life, happiness is not the easiest thing to find; sometimes, it takes significant risks to tackle an opportunity that your gut is telling you is the right thing to do, as if you are being called to pursue it. For some, it can be leaving your past behind and starting a new chapter miles and miles away from home. For others, it could be as small as applying for that job you feel connected to or signing up for volunteer work once a week. However, if you avoid the risk and limit yourself to a lifestyle you think is inauthentic, you will lose the opportunity to grow taller and stronger. The tallest trees have the biggest roots, and the happiest people have learned from many life experiences, both good and bad.

The story you have is in your roots, the more you learn and challenge yourself, the more you have to offer to those who listen as you continue to grow.

Reflection

Please take this time to find a comfortable position to sit in and quiet your mind. Let Erin's story resonate in your heart and reflect on the following questions.

1. In your own words, who are **you**?

2. How does your identity differ from how others perceive you?

3. What can you do to live authentically and genuinely?

Song for Reflection: "Roots Before Branches (Glee Cast Version)" by *Glee* Cast

Chapter 10:
Anna

———

"Everything is going to be okay in the end;
if it is not okay, it is not the end"

—JOHN LENNON

Happiness is *universal*; it can be seen anywhere and on anyone. Despite language barriers, cultural differences, and geographic distance, happiness cannot be wiped away. A genuine smile and a face lit up from joy is a sign of happiness that can be seen by us all. This is an idea that my friend Anna has expressed to me (you might remember her from chapter one, she's the one who told me the icebreaker). To her, happiness is not a feeling that can be described through words, because happiness can be achieved in so many different ways to each and every person. What makes every one of us happy will differ, but the feeling we experience when we truly are happy remains the same.

Anna has learned about happiness being universal through engaging in immersion trips throughout her years in college. Over the years, she has traveled to Guatemala, Nicaragua, and

Cuba with the purpose of learning and becoming immersed in the ways of life of the people in these countries. For many people, going on just one immersion trip opens up your mind to the differences in life that exist around the world, but not Anna. She knew that each country she immerses herself in would offer her a new, unique appreciation of life. Each and every time, she was able to recognize the love and happiness in those around her. The immersion that holds a special place in her heart was her ten days in the gorgeous country of Nicaragua.

To her, Nicaragua offers a sense of serenity like no other place she has ever been. The beauty of the country was reflected in everyone who entered her life during the trip. From the superb sunny days of exploring the beautiful landscape to the friendly faces of those who live there, Nicaragua felt like home. Every road she walked, she was greeted with smiles and waves from those who live in Nicaragua. Behind this door of opportunity, she was welcomed into the country with open arms, truly opening her heart to the kindness of strangers.

During her time in Nicaragua, a memory that always brings a smile to her face is when she had the opportunity to spend time with a native family in the country. Through the short stay, Anna learned about how the simplest things can provide happiness, even when you are in an unfamiliar environment.

Throughout the experience, she was able to stay at the home of a woman who she soon would love dearly. Anna stayed at the house with just one other girl from her university, where they would become a part of the family who lived in the house.

During the time spent at the home, Anna learned how the house mother, or doña, cooked and listened to the many stories she was willing to offer to these two strangers from America. They spent countless hours listening to this kindhearted woman describing her life to then in Spanish, while the girls quickly tried to translate into English to understand.

They felt at peace as this woman allowed them to explore her long life, a life riddled with challenges unlike those we experience in wealthier countries. Despite living in levels of poverty that may be insufferable to many of us, this woman approached each story with a smile on her face and a positive outlook for the future. She had made it this far in life and was happy with everything she had, although it may not seem like much. Although these small interactions may not appear to be significant, the impact of kindness and genuine caring truly shined.

As the days passed, Anna felt her love toward this kind woman grow and respected her vulnerability to share such stories with girls she had just met. However, the time spent at her house soon had to come to an end, causing more heartbreak than expected. Relationships tend to grow strong faster when the distractions of our daily lives are stripped away. With no electronics, cell phones, or schoolwork to take away from the time spent together, Anna felt a raw connection to this woman she had just met.

As the girls were packing up their bags to continue with their trip, they could not help but feel pain in their hearts from possibly never seeing this loving woman ever again. Before they walked out the door, their doña gave the girls a big hug and told them something neither of them will ever forget. Their doña said to them, "This is not a goodbye, but rather a see you later, I know you will come back and visit me again."

Hearing this sentiment made the girls hurt even more as they were walking away from the house. This woman was kind enough to offer her home, food, and support to these two girls she had never met before, ultimately treating them like family. In a country that had unfamiliarity with every turn of a corner, it was easy to feel scared of what may cross your path. This sense of fear was instantly erased by the warmth and love offered by their doña. Despite having very little knowledge on the English language, the doña was able to create a loving environment for Anna and her friend, so much so that she wanted the girls to return to her later in life. Even though they had only known each other for a few days, the relationship that was able to grow out of merely listening to her stories and appreciating her kindness is something that will forever inspire Anna. Love actually does extend past a language barrier.

In fact, the doña was not wrong; Anna had actually been selected to lead the next immersion trip down to Nicaragua in the winter of 2019. However, due to the state of Nicaragua not being seen safe enough for the university, the location was soon switched to Cuba. Rather than returning to seeing her doña, Anna would learn another important lesson about happiness that she may not have been given the opportunity in Nicaragua.

* * *

While in Cuba, she was responsible for taking the photos throughout the experience. With her phone in hand, Anna would soon discover the power of a simple photograph. Anna described the magical moment of "just looking through the lens and catching people in a completely candid moment, and seeing the joy on their face. That is what true happiness looks like."

One of the best things about a camera is that it allows you to capture the raw emotions someone is feeling in that exact moment. Unlike photos that people pose and smile for, candid photos offer the ability to look into someone's real emotions through their genuine reactions. People express their true reactions when they do not think anyone is watching, and sometimes only a flash of a camera can catch this. In these moments is when you see the pure happiness and sense of joy that someone is experiencing.

To Anna, this is exactly what happiness is, the way someone's face lights up and smiles. The way a genuine smile spreads across a face and someone's eyes expand with joy is something that cannot just be put in a sentence. Achieving this type of happiness is not done through a checklist or hitting a certain point in life, but instead can be done through any little moment in life. What makes us happy is unique to us, but the feeling we experience is universal to all.

However, this path to happiness is not always the easiest route and can be overshadowed quickly. Anna loves to help people and see their faces light up with pure joy, but she did not always have this perspective. Very early in her life, Anna faced an obstacle that could have ended her life long before she grew into the loving person she is today. When Anna was only nine and a half years old, she discovered that she had a hole in her heart, a condition called atrial septal defect.[24]

According to her doctor, it was a miracle that the hole was found, or else she would have likely lost her life by the time she turned 18 years old. Many who suffer from the same diagnosis often suddenly die during exercise, leaving nothing but questions and concerns for their loved ones. Hearing this diagnosis and the severity of the condition is enough to fill an entire family full of fear, which is precisely how Anna's family felt.

There were many sleepless nights, and countless prayers said over the health of Anna, hoping that she would be able to live a healthy life. Because the doctors were able to recognize the hole, Anna was able to endure open-heart surgery to save her life. Despite a solution being found, this operation brought even more anxious thoughts to her family. In a scenario like hers where she had to undergo surgery at such a young age, so many factors could go wrong and cause Anna to lose her

---

24 "Atrial Septal Defect (ASD)." Mayo Clinic. Mayo Foundation for Medical Education and Research, January 25, 2018.

life. This thought is something her parents feared every day. A day did not go by where they felt at peace leading up to the operation that would determine Anna's fate. Thankfully, the surgery was a success, and Anna was given her life back after risking it being taken away by a hole in her loving heart.

As life went on, Anna became appreciative of the life she was able to live, thankful that her operation had gone successfully. But this soon began to disappear. As she was attending high school, she developed depression, presenting another obstacle in her path of happiness. During these dark parts of her life, she struggled to find the joy that she once knew so well. Although not a physical hole like before, Anna felt as if there were a part of her missing. The love and appreciation she once felt after getting her life back after surgery was quickly fading. Like a black hole in a galaxy, the light around her was being consumed by the darkness.

The physical pain was not the same, but instead, the mental and emotional distress was what caused her to feel a hole inside her. There were even times she would try to commit suicide, where the weight of the world was too heavy on her heart. She felt that giving up would be easier than trying to rebuild her life to be picture perfect. After one of her attempts to take her own life, Anna had a moment where she realized that her life was not supposed to end yet. If her destiny were to die, either her hole in her heart or her previous attempts of suicide would have ended her life. But she knew that *"there is a reason I am still standing here."* She knew that she was still alive for a reason and that her life had a purpose that she soon discovered to be serving and helping others.

A quote that Anna lives by is, *"Everything is going to be okay in the end; if it is not okay, it is not the end."* This quote has given her the strength to continue fighting any obstacle that comes her way, whether it is a hole in her big heart or depression. Through her strength, she has been able to find that *life truly does get better, and there is beauty to see all around us.* She has been able to continue living her life and finding the happiness that exists inside everyone she meets. Whether it is doctors, her friends, or even a Nicaraguan woman who welcomes strange Americans into her home, Anna has been able to find the moments of pure happiness that assure her that life is more than okay, it is a blessing.

Reflection

Please take this time to find a comfortable position to sit in and quiet your mind. Let Anna's story resonate in your heart and reflect on the following questions.

1. How do you see happiness around you?

2. What types of sights and experiences help you recognize true happiness?

3. How can you spread this happiness?

Song for Reflection: "It's Not Over Yet" by King & Country

Chapter 11:
Barbara

"By facing our challenges and overcoming them, we grow stronger, wiser, and more compassionate."

—JOHN TEMPLETON

The challenges we face are unique to us, but the concept of facing challenges is something we all share. Whether it be facing a divorce, overcoming a battle with mental health, or even as small as going to gym class, challenges come in all shapes and sizes. Unlike in a video game or a reality tv show where people have several chances to win, challenges in our lives continue, even when we might not want them to. We cannot simply give up trying to win, for the obstacle that stands in our way will remain. Even when we do become victorious, there are plenty more challenges lined up in our path for us to face.

However, challenges are necessary for us to grow. If we all lived in a picture-perfect world, how often would we venture into the unknown and leave our comfort zone? How are we supposed to know what we are passionate about if we stick to what we are told and taught?

I want to give a quick example of this using my friend Hannah. This past year, she co-led an immersion trip to the U.S. and Mexico border, surrounding herself with the lives and struggles of those who migrate hundreds of miles to the border. These few days led to developing a passion for humanitarian aid to immigrants. This then led even further to her dedicating the next year of her life, providing humanitarian aid as a young adult volunteer at Tucson Borderlands.

What if Hannah had decided to listen to all the news and politics painting immigration in such a dangerous and negative light? If she had remained in her comfort zone, she might have never discovered this passion.

Challenges push us to better ourselves and realize our potential. We face them in our personal lives, in our workplace, and just about any place we go. There will always be challenges. We can either decide to take an easier route and avoid the issue at hand or brace ourselves to tackle it head-on, grabbing the bull by its horns. With the second option, it opens the door to limitless potential that can arise from stepping outside your comfort zone, which can be seen in the story of Barbara.

* * *

As adults, people tend to hit the point in life where they "settle" with their current job and lose their ambition of finding purpose in their life. That is how Barbara was feeling when she was working at her desk as a writer for women's magazines. Although she loved her job of writing stories, she often struggled to understand the purpose of many of them. She would dedicate vast amounts of time typing each story, making each sentence perfect, only for it to get published and forgotten about within a week.

With this repeating cycle, it became easy to question if the work she was doing was even recognized by the people she was trying to reach. Until one day, while she was typing a story about a topic she cannot even remember, she was presented with a new opportunity, a challenge. Her mind began to wander, and she decided to do some research on a woman named Georgia Tann, a name that was unfamiliar at the time but would create an impact more tremendous than Barbara could have ever imagined.

The story of Georgia Tann was circulating the news, a baby trafficker posed as a social worker. The story is terrifying when one learns of the evil that existed within her. She would visit single mothers who had very young babies and claim that they appeared to be unhealthy or ill in some way.[25] Since the mothers had very little money, Georgia would offer to take the baby to the doctor, an act that one would perceive as kind. However, Georgia would then tell the mother that the baby had passed away, cutting all ties with the mother to sell the baby up for adoption.

---

25 Raymond, Barbara Bisantz., and. *The Baby Thief: The Untold Story of Georgia Tann, the Baby Seller Who Corrupted Adoption.*

However, this was only one of the tactics she utilized to steal. She would steal babies born in mental institutes and jails, those dropped off at orphanages, and would go as far as kidnapping and telling the parent that welfare agents took the child away. As she continued selling these stolen babies on the black market, she would use the money to bribe doctors to tell new parents that their child was a stillborn and then proceed to take the baby, a truly unspeakable act.[26]

The horrors of this story continued to unravel, often leaving Barbara questioning why she accepted this challenge to write on such a gruesome topic. Thousands of babies had been ripped away from their parents and sold into a life with a new identity. However, there was one factor in Barbara's heart that she knew she had to write this story. It was not because she thought it would sell well or become more popular, but rather, her own daughter was adopted. Barbara's heart ached for these mothers and their babies, wondering if her daughter could have been at risk of being stolen as well.

As a mother, Barbara could not imagine the terror that all of these mothers went through who had their babies taken, never knowing the truth about what happened to them. Each child was living a life that was not supposed to be theirs while having no idea of what their life truly could have been without the interference of Georgia Tann.

As she continued investing countless hours into the research, Barbara decided to be a voice for these mothers

---

26 Ibid.

and write a book called *The Baby Thief*. Through her writing, Barbara was able to tell the readers of the great pain that each mother felt as they were robbed of their child. Although not a happy topic, Barbara found her purpose in sharing these stories to bring justice to the mothers who had suffered great pain.

* * *

However, that is only the beginning of Barbara's story. Later in her life, after writing the book, she decided she wanted to continue her passion for helping people spread their stories differently: teaching public speaking to college students. She was drawn to teaching a speech communications class because she identified with the students and the challenges they faced as they were forced to speak in front of a class.

As a child, Barbara would describe herself as "socially inept or shy" and did not want any of her students feeling this way as they were required to take a public speaking class. She understood that great fear or anxiety is often experienced when it comes to public speaking, especially in front of a group of people you may have never met before. That is why she approached teaching in a supportive manner, making every single student feel at ease in her presence. She understood that some students have struggles that stem deeper than only public speaking, so by being kind to them, she could help brighten their day and assist them in facing their challenges.

While trying to create a positive environment, she decided to create a kindness club on campus. She recalled that one of the speeches given in her class that she will never forget was given by an African American student. She was the only woman of color in the class and sat away from everyone else, distancing herself. Later in the semester, she decided to focus one of her speeches around how differently she was being treated around campus based on her skin color.

She was being treated very unkindly around campus, was often exposed to racial slurs, and ultimately not feeling part of the campus community. Every day was a challenge for her to ignore how others treated her. Once again, Barbara felt this emotion of wanting to comfort all her students. Nobody should have to live in a community where they do not feel the love that exists all around them, especially when the negativity consumes the love. Hence, the kindness club was created in an attempt to bring more unity to campus and bring together the many different ethnic groups that exist.

The desire to bring kindness to others, however, did not manifest from thin air, but rather a challenge she endured as a child. Barbara says that this feeling of wanting to make other people happy resides in her based on "her lacking happiness earlier on in her life." Her childhood was very unhappy. At an early age, Barbara developed alopecia areata, an autoimmune condition causing patches of baldness that can overlap.[27] Being a young girl who was balding lead to other children mocking and making fun of her. She was unable to

---

27 "Alopecia Areata." Alopecia areata | American Academy of Dermatology.

keep up with her friends and just felt a significant amount of pain every single day. However, she did not want to burden anyone by sharing her pain with them. As Barbara grew up, she developed this mindset that was shaped from her past: she wants to be kind to others since she knows how painful it can be to be treated unkindly.

While discussing this reason to be kind, she shared this sentiment with me:

> "Kind people are sensitive, and they "get it." They "get" what it feels like to be different and be treated that way. However, not everyone can take a rough, ugly past and turn it into something beautiful for those around them to see. There is an element in people that allows them to bloom out of tough times, that element being *love*."

When we face a challenge that involves being treated poorly or being bullied, there are two routes we can go. The first is letting this challenge defeat us, allowing the hurt to sit inside us and turn our hearts bitter. The other option is allowing it to be released, turning it into something beautiful. When we recognize the love & goodness in our lives, we can let go of a heavy past and truly live happier, not letting a challenge overcome our lives. In other words, **taking this challenge and allowing ourselves to grow from it.**

Despite not having the happiest of childhoods, Barbara later was able to find what makes her happy through those around her later in life. She loves to see those around her happy; she gets a feeling of contentment, knowing that her loved ones are experiencing the happiness she once lacked. Like many people, she wanted to discover a way to experience this sense of joy in her life, which is precisely what she did. By sharing the stories of mothers who lost their children or helping anxious students to express stories of their own, Barbara found her joy. She understood that everyone has their own unique story to tell, and there should not be anything that silences our stories.

No matter the pain, fear, or anxiety that may arise when talking about our challenges, each story has a lesson that will positively impact the lives of those who hear it.

Reflection

Please take this time to find a comfortable position to sit in and quiet your mind. Let Barbara's story resonate in your heart and reflect on the following questions.

1. What is something that is challenging you to grow right now?

2. How will overcoming this challenge positively impact your life?

3. What is a challenge you've faced & defeated that makes you proud?

Song for Reflection: "Rise Up" by Andra Day

Chapter 12:
Maureen

"I am not afraid; I was born for this"

—JOAN OF ARC

"What is our purpose here on Earth?" is a common question asked when confusion and uncertainty stands in the way of us and our passions. It is also the focus of the song "Beautiful Life" by Colony House, a song that questions the search for a purpose or our significance in our one, beautiful life. When I listen to this song, I allow for the music to flood into my ears, blocking out the distractions around me, truly connecting with the lyrics and the meaning behind each word. I invite you to listen to this song now, or after you finish the chapter. One particular verse that has always resonated with me and left me with more questions than answers discusses finding a place where we *belong*.

A place where we belong can be hard to find. Within the past week, I can recall at least 15 places in which I have visited, but which one is the one for me? For many, this place of purpose is often found in the place they work. It is a daunting realization, the idea that work consumes the majority of our lives and plays an immense role in our navigation of life. So, how in the world are we supposed to decide very early on in our lives, possibly even in our teenage years, about where we want to work and start our adult lives? How can we be sure that we are on the right path to finding to find the place we truly belong?

As a business student, I would sit in class and think about my future. Each day, as numbers and formulas fill the blackboard at the front of the classroom, I would find myself worrying and stressing about what happens after college, not allowing the squeaks of the chalk to break my train of thought. *"How can I make an impact?"* is a question I would frequently ask myself while thinking about my future.

* * *

Over the past three summers, my "office" for my job has looked drastically different than what you would expect when thinking of the word "office." There were no computer screens cluttered with spreadsheets or a maze of cubicles that guide from one meeting to another. Instead of desks, we had colored mats, (mine was always blue) clipboards instead of computers, and field trips instead of meetings. Presentations were given through songs, and eating lunch with your coworkers meant eating with a table full of children. In other words, I had a summer job as a camp counselor.

Working at camp was a job that filled my heart to the brim daily. Each morning, I would ask myself how I can help bring happiness to at least one kid that day. Many kids came to camp because their parents had to work all day, and certainly spending their entire summer in a middle school that turned into a camp was not their first choice.

With this mentality in my head, I made it my purpose to create a place where the kids would want to spend their summer, not a place they were forced to go. Over the 12 weeks each summer, that was my answer to the question posed earlier: *what are we doing here?* Having a purpose allowed me to enjoy each day. Rather than counting the minutes until I got to leave, I found myself wanting to work. I was always looking forward to "pranking" my coworker with the children, proving the blue group was better than the green group, and staying late to spend more time with everyone.

As my last summer comes to an end, the sound of children cheering will soon be replaced with the clacking of keys and phones ringing. The faces that surrounded me will no longer be young and full of excitement, but rather a bit older and focused on the pile of work they have to complete. My purpose will transform from creating enjoyment for kids to meeting deadlines for adults.

However, this does not mean I will not enjoy working in offices or for businesses, but I must be willing to accept the experience that this change presents to me. If we stay stagnant in work, not ready to expand our skills and experiences, we may never discover what we are here to do on this Earth. We should not fear the change, but rather embrace it with open arms, even if it seems scary.

* * *

However, there are people around me who always reassure that our purpose in life is not something you can force, but rather it will make itself apparent when the time is right. I recently met a woman named Maureen, who was once in my shoes as well. In other words, she was struggling to understand what she is supposed to do for the rest of her life. Although she now knows what makes her happy when she wakes up for work every day, this was not always the case.

She claims that she "*fell into*" the profession that she currently loves. Several years ago, Maureen was switching denominations, wanting to start in the seminary, and even possibly become ordained down the line. Throughout this process of change, she also had to leave her past occupation behind. While she was searching for jobs, she stumbled upon an opportunity to be a chaplain intern. She felt connected to the role and applied. Thankfully, she got the job.

After spending ten months helping many women in this shelter, Maureen discovered that she loves to help people. After hearing stories of how these women have struggled emotionally and physically, Maureen knew that it was her calling to provide support to those who need it. Perhaps the fact that Maureen also had a path of suffering from domestic violence played a role in her finding her purpose as well. She connected with them and saw herself in the faces of many of the women. The tears, bruises, and fear Maureen saw in each kind face acted as a mirror into her own past.

However, she turned her history into a lifestyle where she would empower these women and remind them of the support they have. Maureen recalled, "If I did not have people in my life who supported me, I could have ended up like those women," which is why she wanted so badly to help them. She knew that having a source of love in a shattered life can make a grand impact, and she wanted to be that love.

This is just the beginning of Maureen's story, the part where she was able to discover what she knew she was on this Earth to do. As her internship helping these women came to an end, she found herself another job in which she was faced with providing support to a new demographic: children.

For the past two years, Maureen has worked as a community mental health worker, which means she visits people in their home communities to administer mental health services to them. This duty ranges from seeing children in their school or visiting families in their houses. Through this job, Maureen visits with children and their parents to ensure that they are getting the right guidance and care. The children she sees vary from having a disability to being raised through neglect and abuse. In many cases, the parents she sees did not have the best childhood either, so it is Maureen's job to open their eyes to a healthier and safer world for the entire family.

Through each meeting, she can end every day knowing that she is creating a safe space for each child to bloom and grow.

However, these meetings are much more personal than merely visiting a therapist in their office. Maureen is entering into a family's home, seeing where and how they live. She becomes face to face with the conflict and insecurity that people have to endure every day. Through these home visits, she becomes exposed to the factors in their lives that may have caused such poor living conditions for their children. One family has to catch three buses to stand in a two-hour line to get groceries at a local food pantry, and then carry them back to their home. She learns of the pain many people have been through, from battles with addiction, losing loved ones to violence, and the constant fear of danger that coexists with living in rundown neighborhoods.

As one can imagine, seeing people struggle in their homes every day creates a mentally challenging work environment. Maureen said, "A lot of people in the mental health field do not like visiting the homes of their patients because it is too stressful." But for her, this job is something that needs to be done. It needs to be done not for the sake of earning money but leaving a positive impact on the people she meets. Maureen could work a job where she dreads waking up for, or she could be investing herself in the lives of others intending to help them.

This experience of helping families, specifically children, has shown Maureen that she feels deeply passionate about advocating mental health through her faith and religion. Although her career path is still in development, she knows that she wants to continue to assist and support those struggling with their mental health. Whether she becomes a chaplain, or priest, or even can offer mental health services out of a parish, she wants to continue fulfilling her destiny. We have seen how faith has helped Mollie and Gianna gain the strength to overcome their battles with mental health, which exemplifies how Maureen dreams of incorporating mental health support into the ministry of the priesthood.

My conversation with Maureen ended with me asking if she has a quote that helps guide her in her life. Luckily for me, she had a deck of cards that all had a different saint or deity, accompanied by a phrase. As she shuffled and sifted the cards, the one she selected was of Joan of Arc, with the phrase:

"I am not afraid; I was born to do this."

Of all the cards she could have selected, this one brought my perspective into her life full circle. Despite the emotional distress that may come with visiting children who have not been shown the proper love or even women who have suffered from physical assault, Maureen knows that she was born to help people. Other people may not want to take on the baggage that comes with the job, but Maureen has realized she truly was born to be this source of support to these struggling women and families. It is her purpose. Although she claims to have "fallen" into this path of work, the world indeed does act in mysterious ways.

We all have a purpose as we exist here on Earth, and **each of our purposes will become apparent with time.** Some may be born with dreams and ambitions of becoming Olympic athletes or doctors who save lives, but many people discover their purpose as they mature throughout life. If you are still searching to discover how to spend your beautiful life, do not panic. There is no such thing as a life wasted; sometimes, it just takes time for us to discover what we are here to do. Although it may not appear so, we all have a place where we belong. Even if it takes years, you will reach a point where you, too, will think to yourself, *"I am not afraid; I was born to do this."*

Reflection

Please take this time to find a comfortable position to sit in and quiet your mind. Let Maureen's story resonate in your heart and reflect on the following questions.

1. What activities or types of work bring you the most happiness?

2. What does it mean for you to have a purpose?

3. How can you unite your passion with what makes you happy?

Song for Reflection: "This Beautiful Life" by Colony House

Chapter 13:
Karen

———

"Helping one person might not change the world,
but it could change the world for one person"

—UNKNOWN

When we look at people who have their purpose in life and have dedicated decades of years to helping those in need, it is often tough to remember that they had to start from somewhere. People typically are not born with the mentality of "I want to change the world and help the poor," but instead, it is learned throughout their lives. It could be through watching others around you engage in service, learning about an injustice from class, or a large variety of different factors. No matter what might cause the spark of interest, it is always accompanied with your heart feeling connected.

By opening our hearts, we can recognize the passion for helping others that exists inside us, connecting on a deeper level with those we serve. All it might take is deciding to try something new, such as working at a soup kitchen one day per week, for you to feel a connection with those around you. This connection is the first step in the development of the passion of helping others. This concept of learning through personal connections is exemplified in the development of a role model of mine, Karen.

* * *

Karen recalls that the spirit of helping others was constantly around her, even as a young child. Her parents were always such loving people, especially to those who might not necessarily be treated with kindness by others. Her father was a well reputable physician in Washington, DC, treating the elite and making money that *some of us can only dream of making.*" However, he used his skills in a way that many others may never even think of; he would treat those who worked for the rich but could not afford an actual visit. He would put in late hours, providing health care to those who were turned away by others due to their financial instability. He would do so because he recognized the fact that not having enough money does not make you unworthy of being treated like a human being. To him, everyone deserves medical attention; putting a price on good health is truly unfair to many.

Along with using his profession to assist the lower class, Karen remembers a specific event in her life where she felt that spark of passion toward helping others beginning to grow. Around Easter time, decades ago, Karen visited an orphanage with her father for him to provide check-ups for the children.

As she sat in the waiting room, she took time thinking of the situation around her. The thought of *"all these children likely have not spent an Easter with their parents"* came into her mind. This thought made her realize how lucky she has been to have had Easter with her parents year after year. At this moment, an idea seemed to click in her head.

Later that night, she had her parents take her to the store to get Easter baskets, plastic grass, and presents to put in each basket. She wanted these orphans to feel the love that she feels every Easter. The following day, her father took her back to hand-deliver the baskets to all the children at the orphanage. She remembers the sense of joy she got from handing out every basket. With each child, she felt a rush of joy that she was not familiar with yet. That being the joy of bringing happiness to others. Not only was she able to spread her love to many children who were at a rough patch of their lives, but her parents were in awe of the compassion Karen showed that day. This feeling of happiness is what has motivated her to continue spreading this love to children today on a much larger scale.

As the years passed, the passion for helping children remained dormant in her heart, waiting for the perfect opportunity to come her way. Little did Karen know, a trip to Honduras would be an experience in her life that would completely change the direction of her career. That is how life works sometimes; some of the most eye-opening experiences occur when you are least expecting it.

Karen and her husband had always taken trips and vacations around the world to explore different cultures. They loved the opportunity to experience life through a different perspective, even if only for a few short days. Each country was offering a new opportunity to learn and grow, but their visit to Honduras in 2003 would leave an impact much larger than the rest.

While exploring the countryside with her husband, they stumbled upon 24 teenager boys that showed signs of abandonment and neglect. At first glance, all she could see were their skinny torsos with ribs poking out, dirty feet covered in cuts, and faces with looks of hopelessness. The sight of these boys was something she will never forget; the extreme hunger and lack of nutrition is something she never wishes anyone would have to endure. Seeing these skinny boys with no food and the hope faded from their faces is a scene that could resonate in someone's mind for a lifetime. These boys showed signs of not eating for four days and likely could have starved if Karen did not stumble upon them.

After introducing herself, she wanted to know what she could do to help and asked, "What are three things you wish you could have at this moment?."

It was impossible to predict what these boys were going to say. They had been abandoned, devoid of the luxuries and necessities that we use in our daily lives. These three wishes that these boys had is what caused the changing point in Karen's life and is what broke, yet opened, her heart. The boys asked for food, shoes, and eleven pencils.

The pencils were for them to teach each other the knowledge they had. In fact, the only way for them to get any education was to teach each other all they knew. After hearing of the lives that these boys had been living, Karen made a promise to them that she will make things better. She did not know how costly it would be to promise healthy lives and education to these boys, as well as the many others like them. However, one thing she did have was a voice, and she made sure that their stories would be heard. Karen often says the quote, "To the world, you may be one person. But to one person, you might be the world," and she wanted to make an impact in these boys' lives.

Fast forward 15 years, and the great strides Karen has made in Honduras are absolutely admirable. Rather than continuing her lavish lifestyle of traveling around the world and admiring art museums across the globe, she gave up that life to make an impact in the lives of others. Karen and her husband created Hope for Honduran Children, an organization that aims to protect, educate, and love disadvantaged and often abandoned children in Honduras, a country riddled with poverty and gang violence.[28] She began spending her money on plane tickets to bring supplies to these boys in Honduras instead of taking vacations. However, this care toward others extends further than merely providing an education; she treats each child as if they were her own.

---

28 "Hope for Honduran Children Foundation." Hope for Honduran Children Foundation

Teaching how to read and write is beneficial, but that service is only short term. Karen personally helps each child along their journey to adulthood, making sure they stay on the right path for a healthy future. Even though she has helped 5,537 children throughout her life, every one of them has a special place in her heart.[29] Despite it being more work than she ever could have imagined, Karen recalls that she would not give up this lifestyle for anything. The joy she receives from making these boys' lives better is a feeling she could not earn anywhere else in life. Unlike temporary happiness, this sense of joy is pure love and will always stick with her.

Helping her children in Honduras is not only what Karen is passionate about, but it also is what brings her great joy in life. Rather than spending her money on expensive vacations as she had once done, she now uses it to better the lives of others. This sentiment of helping others brings her peace and joy in her life, something she always reminds me ever since the first day we met.

Anyone can change the world, even if it is merely just the world for one person. Although Karen had the passion in her heart of helping others as a child, she did not recognize her calling in Honduras until many years after she gave Easter baskets to orphans. **This goes to show that no matter how old you are or what path you have taken in life, it is never too late to make an impact.** You may not be able to provide safety and education to children in Honduras like Karen, but

29 Ibid.

that should not deter your passion. Even if it is an activity such as handing out Easter presents to orphans; you have the potential of changing the world for even one person, making all the effort worth it.

Reflection

Please take this time to find a comfortable position to sit in and quiet your mind. Let Karen's story resonate into your heart and reflect on the following questions.

1. How do you feel when you help others?

2. How do you feel when you are the one being helped?

3. How can you tie helping others in with happiness?

Song for Reflection: "Awake My Soul" by Mumford and Sons

Chapter 14:
Liz

————

"Love and kindness are never wasted"

—BARBARA DE ANGELIS

The next time you are in a room full of friends and family, scan the crowd. Let your eyes fall upon each of the faces, recalling all the memories you have shared with them. With each person you see, ask yourself, *"How has this person helped shape me to be the person I am?"* Some faces may belong to people who have supported you through tough times, others who have just been a kind shoulder for you to lean on. There will also be others who have done much more than the rest, teaching you lessons and leading a life that exemplifies who you aspire to be when you are older.

When I do this activity, one of the people in my crowded room would be my friend Liz, who I had only met a little over a year ago. The best way to describe her is as someone who speaks with such passion and joy that you can see the rays of sunshine within her spread into the world. The first night we met, I quickly realized that I have never seen anyone as euphoric and loving, especially to strangers. As we became closer, I would notice the way her voice lights up with joy, and the tone of her voice reflects the emotions she is feeling. Through this, she truly brings every word she speaks to life. No matter the person, she approaches each conversation with kindness and compassion to make anyone feel truly at home. She radiates a sense of happiness that can be felt by all those around her.

If you are like me, you might be wondering how did Liz develop this appreciation of life and love to all those she meets? What, or who has influenced her that has allowed her to live so happily and joyfully? In simple terms, she acts as a sponge. She absorbs the love, support, and kindness from those around her and allows it to become a part of her. Each lesson she learns from watching those who are close to her are absorbed into her heart, where they will remain and guide her life. To exemplify this, we will need to look deeper into the hearts of the people whom Liz would see in her crowded room full of people, starting with a woman who shares her love with all: her mother.

It may seem cliché to say that mothers tend to be the most caring and loving people in the world, but to Liz, her mother exemplifies what it means to show unconditional love. Throughout her 21 years of life, Liz has grown up watching her mother embrace the world with constant, positive love and encouraged Liz to do the same. No matter who her mother was around, whether it be her coworkers, people at church, or even people she passed at Walmart, her loving personality affected them.

In one instance, Liz recalls being in the car with her mother as she pulled into the Arby's parking lot. Without any hesitation, her mother pulled out an envelope and headed for the door. Inside the envelope was a gift card to The Children's Place. Liz soon discovered that her mother had already been inside earlier and noticed the cashier, a pregnant woman, her tired eyes acting as windows into her weary soul. Her mother had listened to this woman's story, "a woman struggling to afford diapers while only being able to see her husband behind bars." Her mother recognized a struggling soul and wanted to do anything she could to help. To everyone else in that restaurant, the cashier was just a simple worker being paid to take orders, her story and struggles washed away behind the uniform she wears.

This is just one of the many instances in which Liz has watched her mother provide love to strangers, acting as a role model to Liz. For many, it is universal nature to love our friends and family, but extending that love to people we have never met before is unfamiliar. We tend to forget that even though we may have never met a person before, they still deserve to be acknowledged, loved, and appreciated. Watching her mother made Liz realize that she wants to give others these signs of hope, living a life that looks at the world through the lens of love. To Liz, she believes that:

"It is one of the hardest things to do, to love a world that begs you to hate. But, that is the most wonderful thing about it, that it is hard work, and work we ought to be engaged in. I am constantly falling short, but trying, every day I am trying. I am ceaselessly inspired by those who possess a constant loving and positive personality because that is one of the most courageous things to do."

This kindness that Liz strives to radiate is not just shown in daily interactions, but also service where she dedicates her time to helping those in need. Whether it is delivering medicine to children in Honduras, leading a spiritual retreat for college students, or connecting incarcerated youth, Liz expresses her passion for serving others to various communities. To many people, engaging in service may be an exhausting activity, spending hours helping people not to get a single cent in return. Why would anyone want to dedicate so much time to the well-being of others? I asked this question to Liz, to catch a glimpse into the mind of someone who cares more about others than often herself. Her response being:

"Something that continues to drive me is the feeling of being most alive. It is on the days when I am the most exhausted and worn out and burnt out, that I find myself engaging in service, which brings the life back into me. It brings energy back into my heart. What drives me is that nothing in the world seems right to me, without serving others, and allowing myself to be served in return."

This passion for sharing her heart with those in need could stem from the never-ending love from her mother, or perhaps another person she would see in her crowded room: her sister.

Liz grew up watching her sister engage in service in countries such as Jamaica, Mexico, and Uganda. Despite Liz's young age at the time, she knew that she wanted to be like her sister, so willing to give her heart and support to those in need. Liz was entirely and utterly displaced by the passion that she saw radiating from within her sister any time she spoke of the work she had been doing. Liz had recognized the calling that her sister had received to go out into the world to be with others, and knew that no matter where her life would lead her, she would be a woman for others through her service.

A common misconception about doing service is that it is a one-way street, meaning that only those who are receiving the additional care are the ones benefiting. However, Liz has learned that this could not be any less true. Through each relationship she forms with those she meets while doing service, Liz experiences a sentiment like no other. The gratitude and warmth shown from those who she encounters is a form of love that is hard to recreate in ordinary society. It is not just a warm, fuzzy feeling she gains while she is serving others, but a much deeper and meaningful connection. In fact, she remembers one conversation with a young man that has forever changed her.

Throughout her semester, Liz participates in a program called Writers in Residence, where she and others would help facilitate creative writing workshops alongside incarcerated youth.[30] During one of the sessions, Liz sat down next to a boy, whom she refers to as Z, and engaged in a conversation. Most people would stray from this situation, often to avoid the uncomfortableness of talking with someone who has walked such a distinctly different life path than them. Even Liz, who had been working with boys like Z before, felt herself fumbling with her fingers and gnawing on the inside of her cheek. In these moments of awkward conversation, she began feeling "the oceans of divide separating me from someone, wishing I could be given the words, unclothing myself of the awkward separation."

However, Z had not noticed the nervous energy coming from Liz, nor did he reciprocate it. When he opened his mouth to speak, he did not care what Liz looked like or who she was or where she came from. All he cared about was that she was another human being, another image of God. During their time together, Z opened up about his life, sharing heart-wrenching stories of pain, suffering, and violence. As his words filled Liz's ears and heart, she wanted to do nothing more than to "reach into his youthful heart and plant flowers of hope and promise within it." However, merely planting these seeds does not guarantee that the flowers of hope will grow, just like how a promise does not always lead to the

---

30 "Writers in Residence (WIR) Program." John Carroll University.

truth. How could Liz ask this 17-year-old child who is getting another 15-year sentence to continue finding the hope in his life? In her own words,

"This was one of the hardest interactions I have had but also the most meaningful. As he sat in front of me, with brown sunken eyes that did not choose to meet mine, and shoulders that hung low as if they were under some heavy weight, he taught me that I could not fix his life. I should not want to either. All I am called to do is sit with Z and listen, and simply be. He taught me that the meaning of compassion is the "suffer with." I am broken by his pain, and he taught me that we should all be. We ought to pray for the ability to be broken by the pain of our brothers and sisters. It is through this that we discover hope."

As our hearts become broken from pain, we allow them to open up and welcome in all those we encounter. By suffering with others and getting a glimpse at the pain in which they have lived through, we better understand the change that needs to happen in this world. Sometimes all it may take is a warm embrace and an open heart to help lighten the weight of the world that is resting on someone's shoulders. From this conversation with Z, Liz learned that by merely offering yourself as a friend and listening to the stories of those you meet, you can provide more help and love than you could ever imagine. We do not always have to want to "fix" people, but just showing authentic interest in them through kindness may mean the world.

* * *

Through watching her mother share her heart with all she encounters, her sister engaging in international service, and listening to the story of an often-ignored teen, Liz has learned that kindness exists in many forms and can change your life. Extending your heart out to others, even in the smallest acts, allows for yours to grow as well. Author Barbara De Angelis once said, "Love and kindness are never wasted. They always make a difference. They bless the one who receives them, and they bless you, the giver."

Any act, big or small, will make an impact in the lives of others and your own. How can you make your difference?

Reflection

Please take this time to find a comfortable position to sit in and quiet your mind. Let Liz's story resonate in your heart and reflect on the following questions.

1. Who are your people in your "crowded room" who have impacted your life?

2. What is one lesson someone has taught you that has resonated with you?

3. Who do you want to be remembered as?

.

Song for Reflection: "Below My Feet" by Mumford and Sons

Chapter 15:
Mary

"Unexpected kindness is the most powerful, least costly, and most underrated agent of human change."

—BOB KERRY

The stories written in this book come from people who were once nothing but a stranger to me. Whether it was just another face in a crowded room or a kind soul who accepted my request on LinkedIn despite not having a single clue who I am, we all started as strangers. You see, this small act of kindness from a stranger may not seem like much, but it can be the first of many building blocks of a supportive friendship.

Mollie probably had no idea that just introducing herself to me at a bar would lead to a friendship spanning two, almost three years. Alternatively, when Maureen saw my message on LinkedIn, she could have never known that a simple click of the "accept" button could lead to her story being shared in a book. All of our closest friends have started as strangers at one point; we just learned to let them in and take a chance with them. If you think about it, it is rather strange that we all start as strangers?

This act of kindness from strangers, however, is more than just taking a chance to build a friendship or relationship. Sometimes it can be even more meaningful than a loved one doing something nice for you. Our friends and family are almost expected to treat us with kindness and love, hence the saying "that is what friends are for." However, when this support is from a stranger, it comes off as very unexpected. You may ask yourself why someone you have never met before would compliment you or offer to pay for your coffee at Starbucks. In these sudden acts of kindness, we are reminded that there is not only love in the hearts of our friends but everyone around us.

One may argue that thinking this way, that there is kindness in everyone, is as if you are looking at the world through rose-tinted glasses. In other terms, you think more optimistically about the world and the people around you than you should, everything appears to be better than it actually is. In a way, that argument would be right. Not every single person on this planet is going to treat you with the love and respect you deserve. In these instances, whether than dwelling on the negativity, we must focus on the good. No matter how someone treats you, there will always be more good in the world than there is bad. "More good," a simple two words that changed the direction of someone's life drastically for the past three years.

* * *

On December 14th, 2012, a 20-year-old man entered Sandy Hook Elementary school and took the lives of 26 innocent people, 20 of them being children.[31] A woman named Mary was scrolling through her computer at work when she saw this news, and her heart instantly dropped. "How could anyone do such an evil, horrible thing?" she thought to herself as she was refreshing the news website, desperately waiting for more updates on the tragedy. How could she live in a world where the good seems to be fading, being covered by horrible events such as this?

Moments later, one of her coworkers walked into work and handed her a coffee with a smile on his face. Mary looked up, shocked at his demeanor, but accepted the coffee. When she asked how he could be so happy, he told her of a random act of kindness that just happened to him.

"A man ahead of me in line at Starbucks bought a $100 gift card and told the barista to use it to cover the drinks of as many people behind him as he could, in the spirit of Christmas."[32]

This coworker had been facing a very rough year, excited for 2012 to pass and hoped for a better 2013. Seeing how this one act of kindness had impacted him so much made Mary think and question everything. Mary decided to do what

---

31 More Good: Acts of Human Kindness from all 50 States | Mary Latham | TEDxOrientHarbor. 2019.

32 Ibid.

many of us typically do when we need someone to talk to and think things over: she called her mom.

Throughout the course of the conversation, Mary mentioned the act of kindness in the Starbucks. However, the main topic of discussion was the tragic shooting, with Mary repeatedly asking, "How could something so terrible happen?" After going on and on, focusing on the negativity that existed in the world, her mother interrupted, saying:

"You need to focus on the act of kindness that happened... There is always going to be these horrible, tragic things that happen in the world, but there will always be more good, you just have to look for it."

At this point in her life, Mary's mother was battling cancer for the second time. Despite being forced to fight for her life not once, but twice against cancer, her mother was still able not to let the bad in her life weigh her down. This inspired Mary, the idea of looking for the acts of kindness that happen in our lives. She even decided to create a project called the Grattitude (gratitude but spelled like attitude), where she asked people to send in acts of kindness they have experienced through their lives on Facebook. She was excited for the future, to read of the kindness that was being expressed by random people for random people.

Eleven days later, her mother was taken to the hospital for a routine surgery. Hours later, Mary learned that her mother had hours or even a few days at most to live. She sat stunned in the waiting room, feeling hopeless, defeated, and heartbroken. Her mother, the one who lived life so focused on the good, was being defeated by the bad. How could Mary focus on the good when the happiest person in her life was about to be taken away from her? By the end of the week, Mary's mother passed away.

Following the loss of her mother, there were two ways in which Mary could have continued living her life. She could have dwelled on the loss, focusing on the negativity that appeared to be flooding into her life. Alternatively, she could honor the words her mother once told her, that being to continue looking for the "more good" in life. This scenario is something that many of us face in our lives as well: do we pick ourselves up and move toward what will make us happier, or do we take the easy option and continue to fall victim to our negative thoughts. One leads to an endless amount of opportunities but requires great strength while the other allows you to do nothing but remain stagnant in life.

For Mary, the decision took time, but she ultimately knew what she wanted to do: she wanted to honor her mother and remind everyone that there is hope and good out there. On October 29th, 2016, Mary started a journey like no other. She decided to pack up in her mom's Subaru and travel across the country. Her mission was to visit all fifty states to learn of stories of acts of kindness to collect and compile in a book, finding more good to share with everyone.[33]

---

33 Ibid.

However, this was not like your ordinary cross-country road trip. When I say learn about kindness, what I mean to say is depend on the kindness of complete strangers. She had no outlined map of where she was going to stop each night, no hotels booked, and barely any couches lined up for her to sleep on each night. She reached out to her contacts on Facebook, asking for them to ask their friends, family members, or anyone they know across the country if Mary could stay with them. She realized that it is unlikely she will be able to find mutual friends in all 50 states and that she truly will have to trust complete strangers.

Some people might have been scared if they were Mary, worried about their safety in the houses of strangers. Although it is a valid concern, these people would be disobeying the advice Mary's mother once told her, that being to look for the good in all people and all situations. Following this advice has led Mary to over 130 houses to stay in, 44 states, and a constant reminder that there is more good. [34]

Even people she was not expecting to meet with would offer her words of advice and kindness. One that undoubtedly stood out to her was the story of an Uber driver; all told while driving Mary to a coffee shop to hear another woman's story. The driver first arrived in the United States twenty years ago with a friend; they had traveled from Sierra Leone, a country in West Africa. His friend, who was once a doctor in Sierra Leone, had to live in a shelter due to not having a place to stay. He was able to find work, not as a doctor, but as a newspaper boy who would

34 Ibid.

throw newspapers onto the lawns of homes early in the morning. One day during his route, he had thrown the newspaper a bit carelessly, hitting and breaking a security camera.

At this moment, he faced the choice of running from his actions or facing them head-on. He decided to leave a note on the newspaper, apologizing and saying he will come back later in the day to pay the homeowner for the damage. This man who was living in a shelter and the only money he had came from delivering newspapers was willing to pay for a security camera for a stranger.

As he returned later that day, the homeowner invited him in, telling him that he respected his honesty. As they continued talking, the homeowner soon learned of the friend's journey and the struggles he was undergoing, despite his medical background. This homeowner saw the potential in this struggling man; he saw the good. He decided to put him up in a studio apartment and paid his way through medical school, allowing him to become a doctor like he was destined to be.

When Mary heard this story, she was overcome with emotions. She asked the Uber driver why this homeowner would financially help this man so much, despite just meeting him just that day? The driver responded by saying,

"By leaving that note, the friend had done the right thing. He could have walked away, but he did not." The homeowner decided to do the right thing that day, too; he used his wealth to help this man follow his dreams of becoming a doctor."

As the driver pulled up to the curb at Mary's stop, he left her with one more piece of advice, "The most important type of work you do is the work you do with your heart, just like the homeowner, and just like you."[35]

To this day, Mary is still doing work from her heart, telling strangers across the country the simple phrase her mother shared with her that started her entire journey. There is more good. Even in times of tragedy, illness, and heartbreak, Mary is constantly reminding herself that there will always be more good in this world. If we cynically view the world, we limit the opportunities for us to learn and grow from strangers. Every person has a story to tell and a lesson to give, not just our friends and family. A simple hello or a smile can lead to a conversation, which can lead to a story that you will remember for the rest of your life, reminding you that there is more good.

---

35 Ibid.

Reflection

Please take this time to find a comfortable position to sit in and quiet your mind. Let Mary's story resonate in your heart and reflect on the following questions.

1. List as many *good* things in your life as you can throughout the duration of the first song

2. How frequently do you stop and appreciate the gifts in your life?

3. What can you do to see more of the good in the world around you?

Song for Reflection: "There Will Be Another" by Bronze Radio Return

"I am a lighthouse rather than a lifeboat. I do not rescue, but instead help others to find their own way to shore, guiding them by my example"

—UNKNOWN

Part Three:
SMILE

Chapter 16:
Defining Happiness

———

Being the last part of the book, one might think this is the time to finally hear a comprehensive definition of the word happiness, stemming from and connecting all the different stories into one cohesive sentence. However, this would not accurately represent what your happiness may be, nor mine. Happiness is a very customizable term, meaning that it can change from person to person and even day by day, depending on the person you are asking. The fact of the matter is that it is impossible to broadly define the concept of happiness and apply it to every single person. To better exemplify this idea, I had the help of some friendly faces that you met throughout this book tell me their definition of happiness.

At the end of each conversation, I asked every person the same question, "What is your personal definition of happiness?" I decided to ask this question last for two reasons: The first being that if I were to ask it first, the speaker might feel obligated to mold their story into this definition, creating an inauthentic narrative. Instead, they were able to have the details of their unedited, raw story still fresh on their mind while being surprised with this question. Second, I wanted them to reflect on the words they had shared and decide if they were happier now, thanks to their vulnerability, strength, and love.

First came Jamie, the man who helps college students seek happiness. He described happiness according to a scientific model, the PERMA model. This model discusses how happiness stems from positivity, engagement, positive relationships, meaning, and accomplishment. He uses this model often to help students address what they temporarily lack in life.

We then heard from Mollie, the kindhearted friend hiding a dark side of her life. To her, happiness is "fully accepting and loving where you are at and what you are doing." In other words, being "excited about the future, not devastated about the past, and loving where you are currently at." Owning your story, being proud of who you are, who you were, and who you aspire to be.

Following her was Fabienne, the woman who turned divorce into a passion for helping other struggling souls. In her words, happiness can be "enjoying the great moments, and not being afraid when you cannot find the great moments. When it is not so good, knowing how to navigate the low and not fearing the low." Not giving up when things are not going well but continuing to better yourself to find your happiness.

Then came Gianna, the woman who learned to be kind to all she meets, but first had to be kind to herself by lifting her anchor. When asked, she had to think for a moment, and then told me that happiness is "one of those things you do not want to define for yourself. If I define happiness, what if I never meet that standard or goal that I had set?" After reflecting on what she had said, she ended by saying that "Happiness is love, I do not think I could separate the two," which can be seen in how she shows her love so readily.

Next was Erin, the *Glee* fan who allowed her roots to grow, who said the following: "I really think authenticity. I think happiness is when you can look around you and where you are and see how your past has connected to your present. That is when you can see everything is falling into place. Things could be bleak in that moment, but if you know that it is bringing you closer to a goal, I believe you will be able to find happiness."

Then Anna, who captures moments of love and joy with a camera. Happiness, to her, is "when you look at someone and see them in a candid moment, seeing the joy on their face. You can tell when someone is in a pure joyful state. It is not something you can define, but rather you see in people."

Barbara, the writer who has faced many challenges, discussed how she finds happiness through other people, especially family. "Contentment through seeing those I love and see around me are doing well," loving selflessly, which bring joy back to her.

Following her was Maureen, the woman finding passion through her job of helping others, saying that "Happiness is a choice, the personal ability for people to choose growth and finding peace of mind." Merely waiting for things to get better is not the solution; we must choose to seek out what makes us happy.

After her came Karen, the co-founder of Hope for Honduran Children, claimed she strives for joy rather than happiness. "Happiness can be fleeting and temporary while joy is forever, lasting in your soul." We should not aspire for temporary fixes, but rather what makes us genuinely joyous.

Liz, the beacon of positivity and love who learns so much from others, defined happiness as "community, a love-rooted community where no one is too far out of God's reach, or our reach." Not living a life where we live jealously, but rather accept all those around us with open arms.

We finished with Mary, who finds happiness in the kindness in even the simplest of acts from people across the country, especially those who she just met for the first time.

These definitions are not told for you to see which applies best to you or to compare yourself to how others perceive their own happiness. Instead, follow their story and keep their happiness definition in mind, thinking of how they were able to grow and flourish. When it comes to you and your happiness, the only thing that matters is you.

This may appear to contradict the idea of "living selflessly," but one who struggles to love oneself cannot fully love others.

We must fill our own hearts with love to then let it flow freely to all those we encounter. The same can be said about our happiness, that if we parade around pretending to be happy to make others feel better, it is inauthentic. We must be happy with who we are in order to become a beacon of a guiding light, or an anchor, for others.

With the focus being on ourselves, one takeaway that each story teaches is that every single one of us matters. Our stories and our lives are not without purpose, for we all have a reason for being here. **You matter.** These two words may seem cliché, but the impact and truth behind them have significant meaning. No matter what we are doing in life, if we are lost or working toward a goal, our story matters, and so do we. There may be times when you question your existence, thinking you may just be another book on a shelf in a library. As libraries are lined with thousands of books, they each have a purpose to many people, just like us.

I worked as a student librarian at the wonderful Grasselli Library throughout college. Through this job, I learned that no matter how old the book may be, it had always been checked out at least once. There was always at least one person who needed the information that only that one book contained. The content within those pages had positively impacted at least one person who read it. Our stories are no different; we have been writing our life story, day by day, with a purpose.

I ask of you to think about your life and how many people you interact with each day. The obvious faces that come to mind may be family, friends, co-workers, and neighbors. Just your existence has already left a mark on them, likely in a positive way. Even in small interactions, a polite conversation with a cashier, a smile to a person walking by, or a compliment to a stranger, you have made an impact, and you matter to them.

My friend Cait Matt once showed me a quote from Morgan Harper Nichols, urging that we "Tell the stories of the mountains [we] climbed. Our words could become a page in someone else's survival guide." Although meant to be taken figuratively, I decided to take it quite literally and retell stories of the mountains each storyteller had climbed and create my own "survival guide."

Every person I had asked to include in this journey were utterly shocked, thinking that they had little to offer once they heard about the purpose behind the book. In their surprised reactions, I learned that so many of us have no idea of the impact that we are creating on those around us. You never know who may benefit from hearing your journey and how many would include you in their survival guide, looking up to you for guidance and motivation in their own struggles.

We should be proud of who we are and where we come from, even if it is not picture perfect. In other words, owning our stories and sharing the details of the mile behind our smiles is essential. Not only will it lighten the weight of our anchors, but we can make an impact in the lives of so many others.

We all have a story to tell, and we all truly do matter.

Chapter 17:
Owning Our Stories

———

Welcome to the end destination, also known as the end of the book. Along the ride, or read I should say, you met some of the people who have deeply impacted my life. With their own stories and lessons, it may be a lot to take in all at once. I have been alive for twenty-two years and still am letting their lessons settle down in my heart and mind, so I imagine it can be a bit overwhelming to read all these stories back to back. So if you would like, take a moment and pause, listen to a song that resonated with you, and find peace.

* * *

Each of the kind souls mentioned in this book have taught me many different things, but one lesson remains consistent throughout — life gets easier when we do not run from ourselves. I want you to think of all the negativity, pain, and hurt you currently have sitting on your shoulders and weighing on your heart. Now picture that as your shadow. Our shadows are always with us, the dark cloud that drags by our ankles as we walk. No matter what we do, it will always be right there with us; we cannot just run away from our own shadow. The same is true about our past; we cannot run away and hope we can outrun ourselves.

Rather than running, we need to learn to embrace ourselves, even the parts we may not like. What I have learned is that for us to live genuinely happily, we must find the happiness within to then radiate outward. The speakers in this book, some of the kindest and most loving people I know, are at peace despite undergoing great struggles in their past. At first glance, I assumed they were so happy because they did not experience any struggles in their life. But in reality, it was the exact opposite. Despite the pain they faced, and still face in life, they have learned to love themselves and not run away from what brings them down.

When we endure hardship, we tend to bottle it up and keep it to ourselves, hiding it away in our minds as if it were a skeleton in our closet. As time passes, we do our best to forget about the past, yet it remains with us. Each day of running from our story is another day we spend worrying about what others may think of us; another day wasted not truly being ourselves. While first organizing my thoughts about what I wanted this book to be about, I stumbled upon a quote from author Brené Brown that says,

"Owning our story can be hard but not nearly as difficult as spending our lives running from it. Embracing our vulnerabilities is risky but not nearly as dangerous as giving up on love and belonging and joy—the experiences that make us the most vulnerable. Only when we are brave enough to explore the darkness will we discover the infinite power of our light."[36]

In other words, with vulnerability comes happiness. We must understand that any struggles that we have endured throughout our lives are not to be treated as a skeleton that we hide. Instead, they represent an opportunity for us to grow in a plethora of ways. With each failure comes a lesson, each cloudy day comes a sun, and each fall comes a rise. However, they do not come automatically; we have to be willing to make a choice to use our past as a stepping stone, not a roadblock. Whether this means agreeing to see a therapist, opening up to friends, or even making a small, positive change in your life, it is all your choice.

However, this choice does not come easily. As humans, we so naturally stick to our routine, avoiding change, especially if the change involves pushing ourselves to do something new. We become so accustomed to handling issues ourselves, not wanting to reach out and burden others. In the stories we just read, we saw just that: struggling souls who have buried themselves with their problems and weighed down by their

---

36 Brown, Brené. *The Gifts of Imperfection: Let Go of Who You Think You're Supposed to Be and Embrace Who You Are.* Center City, MN: Hazelden, 2010.

anchors. However, we also saw that in that moment where they finally decided to make a change for the better, they were starting their path in living a better, happier life.

In reaching out and opening up about our stories, it opens a window of opportunity to become happier with ourselves. We no longer live life hiding who we used to be, or who we still may be, creating a façade of a perfect life that we want others to think we live. *Happiness is not perfect; neither are we.* Understanding the concept that we cannot live life perfectly and being willing to share our imperfections with others lightens the stress we so often when it comes to living up to expectations. We experience happiness in the authenticity of the lives we are living, not the show we put on for others to watch and enjoy.

* * *

I know I said the stories are done, but I want to briefly mention a few more people who have inspired me throughout the process of writing this book. Each of the following people has followed a passion of theirs to show the strength in stories, embracing their past rather than running. Their lives have been riddled with their ups and downs, but they are living happily, pursuing a dream that helps and lifts others.

Mai, founder of EYEJ: Empowering Youth, Exploring Justice. Through EYEJ, she encourages teens to amplify their voices, engaging in conversations about social justice and the hardships they endure.[37] She reminds every person that their

---

37 "Facts." Empowering Youth Exploring Justice, 2019.

voice matters, and they are more than just a simple statistic. "Youth hold infinite truth and power. Also, many youths do not feel their voices matter, nor are they respected."

Charlotte, creator of Lift Me Up. Her website was created to help make a difference by sharing stories from around the world, in hopes that the words told will echo into someone's life, at the right time. Words have the power to heal, and by sharing stories across the globe, her readers can understand that they can overcome any challenges they face. It serves as a reminder that they can chase their passion and their dreams.[38]

Julia, author of *VulnerABLE: How to Notice the Power of Vulnerability Through Lettuce, Laundry & Love*. Through this book, Julia guides her readers to notice vulnerability and gain the confidence in knowing they are never alone on the path they may be walking.[39] She shares many vulnerable details of her own life to remind us all that being vulnerable is freeing and wonderful.

Josh, founder of Happy Thoughts Candle Company. After struggling with anxiety & depression in the past, Josh wanted to help those fighting a similar fight. He makes and sells candles, then donates some of the proceeds to suicide prevention and mental health awareness. [40]

These four, as well as the many others mentioned in this book, exemplify the belief that owning our stories will better

38 About Life Me Up." Lift Me Up, 2019.
39 Ruggiero, Julia. *VulnerABLE How to Notice the Power of Vulnerability through Lettuce, Laundry, & Love*. New Degree Press, 2019
40 "Happy Thoughts Candle Co." Happy Thoughts Candle Co, 2019.

our lives. Their stories are not hidden away in a closet but are worn on their sleeves with pride.

However, you do not have to write a book or start a business to showcase your story or become happier. The first step in all their journeys has been letting go of what was weighing them down. In other words, the first step you take in conquering the mile behind your smile starts from within. Whether you want to call it an anchor, a cloud, a shadow, or a skeleton in your closet, what weighs you down does not define you. Claiming your victory over your past is not the source of rediscovering the happiness in your life, but it certainly is a good start.

We cannot be happy and love the world around us if we first do not love ourselves. This saying is cliché, but maybe because it has proven to be true for many years.

There are so many beautiful things out in the world to see and explore, but you cannot forget about the beauty that is within you.

Final Reflection

Please take this time to find a comfortable position to sit and quiet your mind. Let **your** story resonate in your heart as you reflect on the following questions:

1. What is your personal definition of happiness?

2. What is preventing you from taking this definition and turning it into reality?

3. How can you overcome this obstacle?

Song for Reflection: "Miles" by Andrew Blooms

The Reading Road Trip Playlist

———

Music is the soundtrack of our lives and played a very important role in the writing of this book. With each chapter, I found myself getting lost in the lyrics of songs to better immerse myself in the story that was being told. Some may have lyrics that relate to the lesson told, while others remind me of the person who first told the story.

Part One: Society

1. "Papercuts" by Tedious & Brief
2. "00000 Million" by Bon Iver
3. "Pretender — Acoustic" by AJR

Part Two: Stories

Calvin

4. "Got It In You — Acoustic" by BANNERS
5. "slow down my thoughts" by Zachary Knowles
6. "Wildflower" by Clay Finnesand

Mollie

7. "Heavy" by Birdtalker
8. "Scars" by I AM THEY
9. "Colorado" by CHAPPY

Fabienne

10. "Be Still" by The Fray
11. "Get Better" by Scotty Sire, Bruce Wiegner
12. "My Blood" by Twenty One Pilots

Gianna

13. "Your Hands" by JJ Heller
14. "There Will Be Time" by Mumford & Sons, Baaba Maal
15. "Who You Are" by Jessie J

Erin

16. Roots Before Branches (Glee Cast Version) by *Glee* Cast
17. "Changes" by Longshore Slim, The Law
18. "In My Blood" by Shawn Mendes

Anna

19. "It's Not Over Yet" by for KING & COUNTRY
20. "Look Up Child" by Lauren Daigle
21." I Will Be Found (Lost at Sea)" by John Mayer

Barbara

22. "Rise Up" by Andra Day
23. "Roll With the Punches" by Colony House
24. "This is Me" by Kesha

Maureen

25. "This Beautiful Life" by Colony House
26. "Show Me What I'm Looking For" by Carolina Liar
27. "My Time Will Come" by Andrew Blooms

Karen

28. "Awake My Soul" by Mumford & Sons
29. "It's Not Right For You" by The Script
30. "Stupid Deep — Acoustic" by Jon Bellion

Liz

31. "Below My Feet" by Mumford & Sons
32. "Looking for Some Light" by Colony House
33. "Give Me Your Eyes — Acoustic" by Brandon Heath

Mary

34. "There Will Be Another" by Bronze Radio Return
35. "Hold Us Together" by Matt Maher
36. "Keep Me in Your Heart" by Warren Zevon

Part Three: **Smile**

37. "Finale (Can't Wait To See What You Do Next)" by AJR
38. "Family / Best is Yet to Come" by Judah & the Lion
39. "Miles" by Andrew Blooms
40. "Moving Forward" by Colony House

Personal Happiness Entries

Here is the entire collection of the personal happiness responses that I received and mentioned earlier in the book. Almost entirely unedited, you can look into how and when happiness is experienced.

> I experience genuine happiness when I'm at concerts. When you're at a concert surrounded by people all experiencing the joy of music and seeing performers live, there is no better feeling. When you're standing there, with friends or strangers, you know everyone is enjoying the moment and forgetting about the world outside. Those are the moments I look forward to and moments that bring me genuine happiness!
>
> —SARAH R

> For me, feeling alive and genuine happiness are synchronous. The moments where my mind is connected to where I am, who I am with, and what I am doing. By being present, I am gifted with joy in all things.
>
> —BECCA F

> I experience genuine happiness when I see others smile and living happily
>
> —MARK A

I feel happiness being around my friends, taking my dogs on a walk, having Sunday morning breakfast with my family, or going to a barre class!

—MAGGIE L

True happiness for me is spending time with my friends and being able to contribute/help others. Whether that is work, service, lending, or verbally.

—NICHOLAS W

I feel happy when I am with my favorite people, eating good food, or doing something I enjoy (reading, swimming, playing a board game, etc.). I know I feel happy because I am smiling or laughing, and my heart feels full and warm.

—MADDIE D

I experience the feeling of happiness when I am doing something that I love, such as working out, hanging out with friends, and being with my family.

—BRETT C

Surrounding myself with my best friends. It doesn't matter what we're doing, as long as we're together we find a way to have fun.

—MAEVE M

I feel the happiest when I am surrounded by loved ones; when we are focused on each other. Whether that place is around a bonfire or in a car or someone's living room, I feel the most at peace with the world around me when I can look around and appreciate the people who I have surrounded myself with.

—ABBY P

When I'm hanging out with friends and while I'm on the golf course. Being outside and with others is how I experience happiness.

—CHRIS S

I feel happiness when I am surrounded by good, genuine people that make me smile, laugh, and feel good about life. I feel happiness when I am able to have real conversations about life with those that I love. I also feel happiness when I am helping others, or making others feel good.

—SAMANTHA S

When I feel happy, it is usually when I am in the full presence of another individual. Someone I can talk to, sit in silence with, have a good time with, or be with for hours. I usually experience the feeling of happiness through laughter and peace but feel it most when I am most fully present in whatever situation I may be.

—NICHOLAS C

I feel happiness when I am at peace with where I am in life. I also feel happiness amongst friends and family, or in one of my favorite places — the beach at sunset.

—ANONYMOUS

I experience happiness when I can see the little things in life working for me. Carrying a perspective of gratitude... through a lens of love for others, has provided me a happier life. I am happy when the song on the radio is a jam, when the sun is shining, and when I am grateful for all I have.

—JOHN T

I experience the feeling of happiness when I am around family and friends. Ideally, in an area I like, such as the outdoors, but ultimately the only thing that is important to me is who I am spending time with, rather than where it is I am actually spending the time.

—OWEN W

I feel happy when I'm at the gym. For me, it is a great outlet for my stress and anxiety. I also love the beach when I can go. I just feel detached from the world I know and truly feel peace.

—ANONYMOUS

I experience the feeling of happiness when I am able to make someone else's day better in a positive way.

Another way that I can experience happiness is through being grateful for all things.

—ANONYMOUS

Being surrounded by those who mean a lot to me. I typically experience in the form of laughter.

—JESSICA C

When I feel appreciated. When I feel loved. When I feel cared for. Nature brings me my purest happiness and sharing that with those I love brings pure joy.

—LAUREN I

I find happiness in a lot of things in life, but the most substantial way I find happiness is through spending time with the people I love. I sincerely cherish time spent with loved ones and friends. Seeing the happiness of others always seems to rub off on me, and spending quality time with friends and family almost always brings me happiness.

—CONNOR F

When I am surrounded by the people I love the most and those who truly genuinely love me back. It's the small moments where everyone is present, not on phones and distracted. Really human connection and good conversation.

—AMANDA C

When I'm outside exploring or with my friends.

—ELISSA F

I feel most happy with my family and friends. Specifically, when we are all together without having to look at our phones.

—ANONYMOUS

I am happy when I am around the ones I love. I am happy when I fully recognize that I am a loved child of God.

—E. M

When I am with people I love; I feel excited and happy to be in good company who appreciates me. I also experience happiness when I am alone and focusing on activities that I love like journaling or reading, things that give me peace of mind and calm me down.

—EMMA B

When I am doing something that gives me value and purpose and giving time to others, I feel most happy.

—ANONYMOUS

I experience happiness when I am around those who I love and care about.

—KAITLYN G

I find happiness most often in the small things, like hearing a soft song coming out of the windows of a neighbor or the quietness of the early morning. From a larger perspective, I am most happy when listening to others talk about their passions, exploring something new, cooking, and writing. I think "how" these feelings come to me is simply by feeling at peace with myself, others, and the environment I am existing in.

—MORGAN G

I experience happiness when I am engaging in any creative activity. Whether it be painting, drawing, playing guitar, acting, etc. I feel most happy when I am doing something that takes focus but is also fun. I am even happier when I do those activities with the people I love.

—ANONYMOUS

I feel happiness when I am surrounded by people who appreciate my talents and value my opinions. I feel genuinely cared for when others voice and show through their actions that they love me for who I am and want to be with me. I felt this feeling through many organizations I was involved in because I learned how to express to others how I can become the happiest in my life.

—ANONYMOUS

I usually feel happiness when I'm with friends or family. We are usually laughing and having fun, or maybe on vacation somewhere. I feel this by a warmth in my heart that spreads to the rest of my body. Almost like a euphoric feeling, I don't want to go away.

—CLARICE A

With my close friends and family when we are laughing together. I also experience it when I am blasting music and driving by myself, as well as when I do something well.

—JACOB F

There are many different times when I believe I experience happiness. It can be when I watch a motivational video online, it can be when I achieve a goal I set out for myself, but I believe I experience the greatest amount of happiness is when I witness the successes of those around me, especially my closest friends. Happiness also comes in different forms. The most common for me is a smile and a laugh. My second layer of experiencing happiness is tearing up in my eyes over a situation I am witnessing or know about. However, I am usually in that moment and not watching it through a screen like I can for a laugh or smile. Finally, the greatest feeling I have of happiness is when I smile, laugh, tear up, and then feel a profound surge of adrenaline throughout my body. That is the best way I can describe it. It doesn't always give me goosebumps, but more of a strong tide of warm energy throughout my entire body, starting at the top of my back behind my neck and moving down through my body into my toes and fingertips. That is the best way I can attempt to describe a truly elusive and indescribable feeling.

—SEAN F

I experience the feeling of happiness when I am with my loved ones, and when I am alone with God. When I am with my friends and family, there is a sense of security and togetherness; it is a shared experience that creates joy through attachment. I also experience happiness when I am alone with God. When I am on a hike/walk or just eating breakfast as I look out the window at passing cars, there is also a sense of quiet security; it's also a shared experience that creates joy through detachment from the world.

—ANONYMOUS

I feel happiness when I am surrounded by a group of people that love, respect and support each other. I feel a great amount of happiness when I make others laugh or when I myself am laughing about something pure and nonjudgmental.

—ANONYMOUS

I usually experience the feeling of happiness when I am with other people, or I accomplish something. I also experience happiness when watching *The Office* or going shopping.

—ABBY C

For me, happiness is when I am with friends or family. Happiness is also when I accomplish something, anytime I can put a checkmark next to a task, I smile :)
—ANONYMOUS

When I am around all of my siblings and their children, which happens about twice a year, I feel energized by intense feelings of love and joy that are overwhelming and that I believe contribute to true feelings of happiness. The feeling is so strong and so energizing that the time goes by in a blur and even though they are my happiest times, I find myself forgetting much of what happened.
—ANONYMOUS

Creating new memories with my loved ones
—ANNA D

Laughing and spending quality time with the people that matter the most to me (friends and family)
—KATRINA M

I smile and feel excited when I see someone that I love!
—LEXIE D

I experience the feeling of happiness when I feel like I'm living fully alive — that I am noticing and appreciating all of the goodness in the people and moments around me and knowing that I am giving them the fullness of myself.
—CAITLIN M

Outside in company, exploring!

—ANONYMOUS

Bed after a long day of work

—ANONYMOUS

I feel genuine happiness in the split second when I'm surrounded by people I love and that love me and I forget what I've been worrying about. And when something I've day dreamed about/had anxiety about comes true. When I can laugh in my anxiety's face because something went my way and wasn't a disaster.

—VALERA G

I experience happiness when there are no current stressors or noticeable problems that are affecting me at the current moment. Aka when things are "just fine"

—ANONYMOUS

I experience happiness when I am fully invested in the present and surrounded by love.

—DANNY D

I think that I experience happiness throughout the entire day and in different circumstances. I feel extreme happiness when my friends and family surround me because I can just feel their love. I also feel happiness when I accomplish work goals or even personal goals that make me proud of who I am.

—AINSLEY G

I most obviously experience the feeling of happiness when I feel free. When I free myself from others' thoughts, from obligations that can wait, from time wasted on my phone, from thinking I am not productive enough, or from trying to be someone other than genuinely me. I do this by spending time with those in my life that I can't help but smile when I see. I also take time away from my phone, often intermittently deleting social media, to appreciate myself and my life as it is. In these times, I like to be in nature or listening to music while allowing myself to express gratitude for all things, good and seemingly bad, in my life.

—REGINA S

I experience happiness when I feel true, positive interactions with others. Whether it is having a deep conversation, learning more about them, being able to teach them something, or even just laughing about something that is something we both relate to.

—ALISON R

When I am with people I love. How- when I experience positive experiences and happy thoughts

—MARIA A

I feel that I experience happiness when I see happiness in others. I especially feel it when I know I had a hand in their happiness.

—ANNA M

Acknowledgments

The process of writing a book is not one walked alone. Not for me, at least. There are hundreds of people I could thank for their time, support, wisdom, and kindness. Although I will not be thanking hundreds, I would like to apologize in advance for how many people I will be thanking in this section.

The earliest thank you I want to offer for this book goes to my fourth-grade teacher, Mrs. Gossett. While I was in her class, my friend, Sean Martinez, and I wrote a book called *Lucy and Sue*. It was an exact replica of *Aladdin*, but with two sisters as the main characters and a much less original plot. Despite this, Mrs. Gossett saw how much time we put into it and allowed us to read the first chapter out loud to the class. Mrs. Gossett, thank you for showing me that there will always be people who support me in what I do. Your impact is not lost nor forgotten, and neither are you.

Another thank you to Julia Ruggiero and Katie O'Connell for publishing their own wonderful books and paving the road for me regarding this whole process. You two women are absolutely inspirational and will change the world in your own unique way.

Thank you to Jessica Cook, author of *OWN IT!*, also known as my partner in crime throughout the publishing process. Thank you for being my rock and putting up with me as we both navigated our ways through our books. It has been a long, winding road, but we finally made it.

Thank you to New Degree Press for giving me this opportunity even to write a book! Special thanks to all the wizards behind the curtain: Professor Koester, Brian Bies, Jordan Waterwash, Stephanie McKibben, Bogna Brewczyk, and Gina Champagne.

Thank you to my best friends, Becca Fortsch, Sarah Reynolds, and Mark Anton, for being there for me and helping me become the person I am today. Who would have thought an accounting study group would blossom into such a wonderful friendship.

Thank you to my M37 family for guiding me with love. It was through your strength, courage, and love I was able to write this book.

Thank you to my grandparents for instilling the value of serving and helping others into my life at an early age. Helping out at Urban Ark every summer taught me a lot about humanity and service, thank you.

Thank you to my family, Mom, Dad, Austin, Justin, Ava, and Woody, for your unconditional love and support.

Thank you to those who took the time to talk with me regarding this book, including: Jamie Greenwolf, Mollie Zoul, Fabienne Slama, Gianna Baker, Erin Buttars, Anna Masica, Maureen Wood, Barbara Raymond, Karen Godt, Elizabeth Marcelli, Mary Latham, Tina Facca-Miess, Mariah Webinger, Sherri Crahen, Mai Moore, and Alia Lawlor.

Finally, thank you to everyone who helped make this book possible by pre-ordering a copy and spreading the word. Thank you for helping me follow a life-long dream; it truly wouldn't have been possible without you. I will forever be grateful for your generosity:

Abby Cacchione	Hannah Singerline	Nicholas Cooke
Ainsley Gialamas	Jacob Schupp	Nicholas Wilson
Alexandra Weber	Jennifer Muckley	Pam Rosenberger
Amy Long	Jeremy Snee	Regina Iafelice
Anne McGinness	Jessica Cook	Richard & Christine
Anne Monnin	Joey Adams	Hutcheson
Annina DaFonseca	John Hupka	Richard Landoll
Ben Skovira	John Tucci	Rob Durand
Bob Faber	Julia Rauhe	Ryan McGowan
Caitlin Matthews	Kaitlyn Grady	Sabrina Almashni
Calvin Chmura	Laura Matteo	Samantha Spencer
Chad Kanakkanatt	Mai Moore	Sarah Reynolds
Clarice Aquila	Margaret LaForce	Sean Cain
Dan Piero	Mark Anton	Sean Freeman
Elizabeth Evankovich	Mark Grabowski	Sophia Rodgers
Elizabeth Marcelli	Matt Grazia	Stacey DeHoff
Eric Koester	Matthew Rombalski	Susan Gesualdi
Fran Miller	Morgan Might	Tess Mattison
Gianna Baker	Nicholas Bucello	Tina Miess

With special thanks to:

Becca Fortsch   Mark Belgya   Marty Long

Beverly Belgya   Gianna Baker

Thank you again to everyone who has supported me along this wonderful path, as well as anyone who picks this book up and gives it a chance. Thank you for joining me on *the Mile Behind the Smile*.

References

Introduction

1. Berry, William. "You're So Selfish." *Psychology Today.* Sussex Publishers, April 19, 2016. https://www.psychologytoday.com/us/blog/the-second-noble-truth/201604/youre-so-selfish.

Chapter One

2. Paresky, Pamela B. "Miserable and Middle-Aged? Is Something Wrong with You?" *Psychology Today.* Sussex Publishers, April 27, 2018. https://www.psychologytoday.com/us/blog/happiness-and-the-pursuit-leadership/201804/miserable-and-middle-aged-is-something-wrong-you.

3. Sturt, David, and Todd Nordstrom. "10 Shocking Workplace Stats You Need To Know." *Forbes.* Forbes Magazine, March 8, 2018. https://www.forbes.com/sites/davidsturt/2018/03/08/10-shocking-workplace-stats-you-need-to-know/#3138c0a0f3af'

4. Hoomans, Joel. *35,000 Decisions: The Great Choices of Strategic Leaders.* 35,000 Decisions: The Great Choices of Strategic Leaders. Roberts Wesleyan College, March 20, 2015. https://go.roberts.edu/leadingedge/the-great-choices-of-strategic-leaders.

Chapter Two

5. "Happiness — Dictionary Definition." Vocabulary.com. 2019. https://www.vocabulary.com/dictionary/happiness.

6. "How the Heart Works." National Heart Lung and Blood Institute. U.S. Department of Health and Human Services. https://www.nhlbi.nih.gov/health-topics/how-heart-works.

7. Sparacino, Bianca. *The Strength in Our Scars*. Thought Catalog, 2017.

Chapter Three

8. Eadicicco, Lisa. "Americans Check Their Phones 8 Billion Times Per Day." *Time*. Time, December 15, 2015. https://time.com/4147614/smartphone-usage-us-2015/.

9. Silva, Clarissa. "Social Media's Impact on Self-Esteem." *HuffPost*. HuffPost, February 22, 2017. https://www.huffpost.com/entry/social-medias-impact-on-self-esteem_b_58ade038e4b0d818c4f0a4e4

10. Kross, Ethan, Philippe Verduyn, Emre Demiralp, David Seungjae Lee, Natalie Lin, Holly Shablack, John Jonides, and Oscar Ybarra. "Facebook Use Predicts Declines in Subjective Well-Being in Young Adults." PLOS ONE. Public Library of Science, August 14, 2013. https://journals.plos.org/plosone/article?id=10.1371/journal.pone.0069841&mbid=synd_msnhealth.

11. Hunt, Melissa G, Rachel Marx, Courtney Lipson, and Jordyn Young. "No More FOMO: Limiting Social Media

Decreases Loneliness and Depression." *Journal of Social and Clinical Psychology*, 2018. https://guilfordjournals.com/doi/10.1521/jscp.2018.37.10.751.

12. Fersko, Henry. "Is Social Media Bad for Teens' Mental Health?" UNICEF, October 9, 2018. https://www.unicef.org/stories/social-media-bad-teens-mental-health.

13. "How Technology Impacts Sleep Quality." Sleep.org. https://www.sleep.org/articles/ways-technology-affects-sleep/.

14. "#Bodypositive: A Look at Body Image & Social Media." FHE Health — Addiction & Mental Health Care. FHE Health, November 30, 2017. https://fherehab.com/news/bodypositive/.

15. Society, American Physiological. "Though Distracted by Social Media, Students Are Still Listening." Though distracted by social media, students are still listening. Phys.org, April 13, 2018. https://phys.org/news/2018-04-distracted-social-media-students.html.

Chapter Four

16. Brown, Brené. "The Power of Vulnerability." *YouTube*. Ted, January 3, 2011. https://www.youtube.com/watch?v=iCvmsMzlF7o.

The Stories

17. O'Connell, Katie. *Live LIVE!* New Degree Press, 2019.

Chapter Six

18. "Manresa Retreat." Campus Ministry. John Carroll University. http://sites.jcu.edu/campusministry/about/retreats/manresa-retreat/.

19. Winch, Guy. "The Important Difference Between Sadness and Depression." *Psychology Today*. Sussex Publishers, October 2, 2015. https://www.psychologytoday.com/us/blog/the-squeaky-wheel/201510/the-important-difference-between-sadness-and-depression.

Chapter Eight

20. Fredrickson, Barbara. "The Broaden-and-Build Theory of Positive Emotions." The Royal Society. University of Michigan, August 17, 2004. https://www.ncbi.nlm.nih.gov/pmc/articles/PMC1693418/pdf/15347528.pdf.

21. Ibid.

Chapter Nine

22. Joyce, James. *Dubliners; A Portrait of the Artist as a Young Man*. New York: Barnes & Noble, 1992.

23. Ibid.

Chapter Ten

24. "Atrial Septal Defect (ASD)." Mayo Clinic. Mayo Foundation for Medical Education and Research, January 25, 2018. https://www.mayoclinic.org/diseases-conditions/atrial-septal-defect/symptoms-causes/syc-20369715.

Chapter Twelve

25. Raymond, Barbara Bisantz., and. *The Baby Thief: The Untold Story of Georgia Tann, the Baby Seller Who Corrupted Adoption*. New York: Union Square, 2008.
26. Ibid.
27. "Alopecia Areata." Alopecia areata | American Academy of Dermatology. https://www.aad.org/public/diseases/hair-and-scalp-problems/alopecia-areata.

Chapter Thirteen

28. "Hope for Honduran Children Foundation." Hope for Honduran Children Foundation. https://www.hopeforhonduranchildren.org/.
29. Ibid.

Chapter Fourteen

30. "Writers in Residence (WIR) Program." John Carroll University. http://sites.jcu.edu/pjhr/pages/additional-links/john-carroll-writers-in-residence-wir-program/.

Chapter Fifteen

31. More Good: Acts of Human Kindness from all 50 States | Mary Latham | TEDxOrientHarbor. 2019. *YouTube. https://www.youtube.com/watch?v=rJLuBqd0a78*
32. Ibid.
33. Ibid.
34. Ibid.
35. Ibid.

Chapter Seventeen

36. Brown, Brené. *The Gifts of Imperfection: Let Go of Who You Think You're Supposed to Be and Embrace Who You Are.* Center City, MN: Hazelden, 2010.

37. "Facts." Empowering Youth Exploring Justice, 2019. http://eyej.org/facts/.

38. "About Life Me Up." Lift Me Up, 2019. http://thisisliftmeup.com/about/.

39. Ruggiero, Julia. *VulnerABLE How to Notice the Power of Vulnerability through Lettuce, Laundry, & Love.* New Degree Press, 2019.

40. "Happy Thoughts Candle Co." Happy Thoughts Candle Co., 2019. https://happythoughtscandlesco.com/.